COSTUME
SINCE 1945

COSTUME SINCE 1945

Couture, street style and anti-fashion

DEIRDRE CLANCY

HERBERT PRESS

Copyright © 1996 Deirdre Clancy
Copyright under the Berne Convention

First published in Great Britain in 1996 by Herbert Press,
a division of A & C Black (Publishers) Limited,
35 Bedford Row, London WC1R 4JH

House editor: Brenda Herbert
Designed by Pauline Harrison
Set in Perpetua and Gill Sans
Typeset by Nene Phototypesetters, Northampton
Printed and bound in Hong Kong by South China Printing Co. 1988 Ltd

A CIP catalogue record for this book is available from the British Library

ISBN 1–871569–83–4

Contents

Foreword

Deirdre Clancy is 'good at clothes' because she is good at people.

Her encyclopaedic knowledge of dress, her rigorous research, her diligence in execution, her inspired drawings, her instinct for the right material, the affection and respect, nay awe, in which she is held by cutters and makers alike, her years of experience across the globe in every medium, all this contributes to her greatness as costume designer; but the secret ingredient is a chemical gift based on an uncanny insight into people, whether it be into fictional characters or the personalities of actors and actresses.

And she brings all this talent to bear upon this treasure-trove of a book.

Start with the drawings: there is a whiff of authenticity that comes not just from her depth of knowledge, but from an understanding of humanity. Each one is a witty take on a human being and each one tells a story. They are deadly accurate, but totally original.

Next, delve into the text. It's quickly apparent that she has written an essential reference book, not just for those interested in the past but for the present also. It's loaded with information, which is all delivered in Deirdre's wry, direct and amusing manner. Most interesting to me are her easy and very accurate connections between dress and society. Back to people again.

A wonderful book, that stands proud from the over-full shelf of dry reference books.

ADRIAN NOBLE
Director, Royal Shakespeare Company

Introduction

To view the recent past, the past of living memory, as history is a peculiar exercise. Memory may not be very reliable, but it can add unexpected insights to otherwise dry research.

The half-century since the end of World War II has seen the most rapid changes in technology, communications and life style the world has ever known. These changes have been reflected in the world of fashion and in the clothing industry – which are not the same thing at all. Long periods of right-wing government in Britain and the USA have had the effect of creating almost as great a divide between rich and poor as existed at the beginning of the twentieth century. However, in real terms, and owing largely to the industry's use of cheap immigrant labour, it is now possible to dress fashionably for less than ever before. Many ordinary people in the West do have more disposable income than before the war, and a large percentage of this money is spent on clothes. And at all levels, clothes are now more likely to be discarded after one season in favour of the newest trend, rather than being maintained or adapted as formerly.

While clothes in the West differ in many ways from those worn fifty years ago, three particular changes strike me as fundamental. Firstly, even the most utilitarian garments are now available in bright colours; everything from wellington boots to overcoats can now be bought in all the colours of the rainbow, whereas previously only neutral shades were available.

The second major change can be summed up in a single word – Lycra. This wonder fabric was initially discreetly introduced in the sixties as a hard-wearing and washable elastic material for ladies' support garments. Bras and girdles were suddenly far more long-lasting and comfortable than before. During the 1980s scientists discovered how to combine Lycra with many other fibres. Combined with nylon or acetate it revolutionized sportswear, and within a short time it was added to the most unlikely fabrics, including denim and corduroy, and used for jeans or skirts.

Lycra, or Spandex as it is known especially in the US, meant that a skin-tight fit could be achieved without complex and expensive seaming. Body shaping, either by weight-training or by a variety of keep-fit regimes, became a new popular obsession, and how better to show off your newly-honed muscles than by encasing them in a brightly coloured, tightly fitting second skin. Personally, I would be happy if Lycra were confined to the gymnasium or the stage. The average bulk of human beings seems to increase year by year, and in many cases it would be kinder to all parties not to wear quite such revealing garments.

The third change is more difficult to define, but is perhaps the most profound. Until the end of the fifties, fashion as understood by the couturiers of Paris or Milan had always been the prerogative of the rich adult female and followed a rigid pattern. Twice a year the established designers held a major show, primarily for their wealthy personal clients, but increasingly for the department-store buyers and the fashion press. Each season the store buyers would choose what they perceived to be the most popular styles to be manufactured for their shops where the new garments would be purchased by slightly less wealthy women. Journalists would bring home sketches and, later, photographs of the new fashions, and in the women's magazines such as *Vogue* and *Harper's Bazaar*, editors would demonstrate the shape of the season, with quite bossy instructions on how to achieve the required look, and how to update last year's clothes to render them acceptable for another season. In the 1950s the great Parisian houses such as Dior, Balenciaga and Balmain exerted a tyrannical stranglehold over what was deemed 'fashionable' and what was not. The only women who rebelled were those who considered themselves too old to bother, too creative to be bullied or too fat to adapt to the new shapes. Of course, many women simply could not afford to keep up with fashion, but as far as the trade was concerned they didn't count.

During the 1960s a radical shift occurred. Quite suddenly, or so it seemed, it was fashionable to be very young. Youth Culture had arrived, with its noisy music and rebellious attitude. The world of high fashion was increasingly out of touch, it was perceived as stuffy, bourgeois, middle-aged and, if anything, slightly silly. The next thirty years saw an increasing fragmentation of the strands of fashion, and in this small book I have tried to make some sense of the way clothing in the final years of the twentieth century has developed. As the couturiers lost their power, the main impetus came from the people themselves. 'Street clothes' became the dominant force, with the couturiers now using styles discovered on the high street, or in the clubs, raising their status (and their cost) by redefining the ideas in expensive fabrics and showing them on skeletal super-models, thus rendering the original street styles out of date for the fashionable young who quickly adopted some newer and more outrageous image.

Meanwhile, many people simply ignore what they consider to be the whole silly business, getting on with their lives in rather simple, comfortable clothes usually purchased from a department store or high street chain, and wearing particular styles for their various activities. Suitable sportswear for cycling, keep-fit, jogging and the ever-increasing range of leisure activities, and occasion wear for formal occasions such as weddings, dinner parties and visits to the theatre now make up most people's wardrobes.

It may be easier to understand the process if fashion is thought of as moving in three separate strands, each one having a different rhythm. The first is high fashion as it is usually understood, couture-led or street-led, but changing every season in an ever more frantic search for something new. The second strand is composed of the clothes the majority of people actually wear. Although influenced by strand one, these styles change much more slowly, with a greater sense of continuity from one year to the next. The third strand consists of an ever-shifting group of what social anthropologist Ted Polhemus calls 'style tribes' or anti-fashion. Occasionally the style of some currently trendy group or other is incorporated into the mainstream, as happened recently with Grunge, and as happens every five years or so with Western-style clothes, but on the whole the tribe, be it Punk, Hippy or Leather Queen, gets on with its chosen life style regardless of fashion, mainstream or otherwise.

In the following pages I have tried to select a cross-section of these three strands from each five-year period since 1945. (This may seem an arbitrary and artificial division of time, but it is surprising how appropriate it has proved to be.) This will, I hope, be useful to fellow designers, theatre and fashion students, interested amateurs, and indeed anyone who has a desire to understand clothing in the second part of the twentieth century.

There is so much available material that it is very difficult to decide on a pure line among the mass of details, and it is in order to find some sense of direction, and some understanding of the endless variety, that I have tried to indicate in the illustrations *who* is wearing what, and what class and manner of person is presented. A true cross-section of each period has involved considerable use of politically incorrect stereotyping of human beings according to age, race, sex, class and occupation. I am afraid it cannot be helped; this is after all a text-book and I can only stress that all descriptions should be appreciated in a spirit of academic enquiry rather than as in any way a criticism of the wearer.

CHAPTER I

1945–50 – Peace and the New Look

Four years before the end of the war in 1945 Britain had introduced the Utility Scheme to ensure that the few available resources would be used economically to produce good clothes. Couturiers such as Hardy Amies and Molyneux chose prototypes that conformed to government regulations limiting the amount of material for each garment, the quality of the fabric, the length and fullness of the skirt. In consequence, great attention was paid to details such as the colour of the piping, a carefully positioned pleat, topped by a mad little hat trimmed with unrationed milliner's veiling. Everyone was encouraged to 'make do and mend', and younger brothers and sisters were dressed entirely in 'hand-me-downs'.

In the United States, where there were far fewer constraints, fashion developed further along pre-war lines. Full skirts swirled out from small gathered waists with fitted bodices, worn with nylon stockings, high-heeled shoes in bright leather, straw hats and matching gloves. Such clothes, so cheerful and so new, were the envy of Europe.

When clothes rationing in England failed to be relaxed in line with post-war expectations the public mood changed to one of impatience and resentment. Matters were made worse by regulations in the late 1940s that allowed British Designer fashions to be exported, but forbade their distribution in England. Economist and broadcaster Louis Stanley called the situation the 'second Battle of Britain' and said, 'It is bad enough when such goods do not exist, but to learn that they are being produced, the best this country can make, but not for domestic consumption is a bitter pill ...' Women were further exasperated by illustrations in the Press showing exotic fashions in Paris, Brussels, New York, Stockholm, even Germany.

The long-term effect of the war years on the garment industry was to establish the concept of mass production. The experience gained from the endless manufacture of uniforms forced the ready-to-wear industry to develop stable patterns of manufacture and distribution that underpin the trade to this day. It is salutary to remember that the clothing industry is the third largest industry in the western world in terms of employment and turnover.

New York designers became far more independent as a result of the wartime severing of transatlantic communications. No longer relying on Paris for inspiration, and led by the brilliant Claire McCardell, they invented the American Look. Sporty, relaxed, comfortable, with clean functional lines as a clear expression of life style, these deceptively simple designs became instant classics, and remain effective, inspiring and fashionable to this day.

As yet, no post-war look had evolved, though there were signs, as James Laver, one of the most clear-headed writers on clothes fashion, commented: 'Fashion has reached one of those turning points in history when everything may happen just because anything may happen to the world.'

What happened was brought into focus on 12 February 1947 in the Paris salon of Christian Dior. For a decade the silhouette of women had remained unchanged. Rationing and the privations of war had imposed a straight, abbreviated, square-shouldered shape, and any deviation was seen as unpatriotic extravagance. It is impossible to over-estimate the impact of Dior's momentous collection. His tall slim house models must have looked like creations from another planet. The mannequins had soft natural shoulders, a wasp waist, a bosom subtly padded for a more feminine shape and rounded hips that were emphasized by shells of cambric or taffeta stitched into the lining. The full skirt exploded into pleats from under the peplum of the jacket or was stitched flat over the hips, and for daytime stopped twelve inches from the floor to reveal sheer stockings and delicate high-heeled shoes. These swirling skirts could have 15 to 25, even 30 yards (12–25 m) of fabric, in itself a sinful extravagance to women who for years had made do with 2½ yards of 36-inch wide utility tweed.

The governments of both the UK and America did their best to dissuade women from wearing the New Look, backed up, oddly, by some reactionary ladies in Texas and Atlanta who formed The Little Below the Knee Club on grounds that it was unpatriotic and unemancipated; but on this issue women were rebellious and unmoved. The shops on both sides of the Atlantic were soon full of the new styles and any manufacturer who had the misfortune to have over-stocked with forties man-tailored suits lost a great deal of money, for nobody wanted them.

Men didn't have fashion in the late forties – they just had clothes, in many instances the same civilian garments that had seen them through their off-duty moments during the war or that utilitarian garment the demob (or demobilization) suit issued to ex-service personnel. Men wore dark, two- or three-piece suits to the office and a tweed sports jacket and flannel trousers at weekends. Young people wore scaled down versions of their parents' fashions. The teenager was not invented until early in the following decade in the USA.

Post-war Britain

1–5   This group is taken from a street party to celebrate the end of the war in 1945. The people are working-class Londoners, for whom fashion, as distinct from clothing, was an unaffordable luxury, even assuming they had sufficient coupons.

1   Young boy. Shorts suit in school serge or flannel. English and European boys usually wore shorts till puberty – or until they reached a certain height. Frozen blue knees and wrinkled knee-socks were common until the advent of elasticated tops to the socks in the late fifties. The shirt is worn open at the neck, over the jacket collar – in a way that would have been disapproved of by the upper classes. The jacket is cut in the style common to all men from the forties onwards – three buttons, small shoulder pads; and the shoes, polished for the occasion, are ordinary laced Oxfords. The outfit is completed with a home-knitted V-neck jumper.

2   The man's lapels and roomy trousers suggest a pre-war suit. The V-neck pullover is endearingly tucked into the trousers, still braced and with turn-ups. The only concession to modernity is a cheery tie, wide and brightly patterned in a 'cubist' style.

3   This lady is something of an archetype. She wears a printed blouse and an old wool skirt. The overall in much washed printed cotton is an almost permanent fixture. The Victory tea was for the children, after all, and washing the dishes had to be done by hand. She wears her good cloth coat, which might have been purchased new, but was more likely bought second-hand in one of the many street markets. Darned rayon stockings and sensible shoes complete her outfit.

4   Her friend looks rather more *en fête*. The beret and the jaunty checks on her tweed coat are stylish, and she has taken her apron off. Otherwise the short-sleeved jumper and skirt are almost a uniform.

5   The girl, perhaps fourteen, is wearing a small adult's Utility suit in its most basic form, with check open-neck blouse, white socks and laced shoes.

6 and 7   Leisure-wear was a very new and American concept. These examples are from the Sears Catalog, the bible of middle America. She wears dungarees over a neat print shirt, and wedge-heeled shoes. The garden trowel shows that such practical clothes in washable fabrics were to be worn for suitable feminine hobbies rather than display, but such garments would win the day in time. He

1

2

3

4

5

6

7

8

9

wears a slubbed cotton two-piece. The shirt is cut straight, so that it can be worn outside the 'pants' (American for trousers) as a cool summer suit.

8   It is difficult to believe that this lady's outfit belongs to the same period as the others on this page. This is Dior's 1947 New Look. The corseted waist, natural shoulders and long draped skirt are for conspicuous display only.

9   An excellent example of a New Look suit modified for real people. In 1948–9 almost every young woman of any means at all would have possessed such an outfit for formal day wear. The neat jacket with set tailored sleeves and nipped-in waist came in all sorts of variations on the same basic shape. The full gored skirt would be about 30 cm (10–12 ins) off the ground. The colour and style of the carefully matched accessories could vary. The whole effect was demure and lady-like.

The English professional classes attend a wedding, 1949

1   Nanny. I do wonder how many people on this page are wearing clothes bought or made especially for them. Nanny's good coat was made for a much taller woman, see the hand-sewn hem line. She wears this classically tailored overcoat in sensible dark brown or grey, with a round-neck, possibly hand-knitted jumper. The low-heeled shoes are enlivened by fringed tongues, which together with the straw loops on her hat are the only touches of frivolity on this rather grim outfit.

2   A classic image of British middle-class childhood, complete with velvet-collared Harris tweed coat, white ankle socks and Start-Rite strapped shoes.

3   Another lady whose smart cream coat was too long and has been turned up. Her hat is stylish too, a kind of enlarged beret with a fringe on.

4   The boy's mother. It is difficult to see that this actually very pretty woman is still under thirty, given her somewhat depressing clothes. I know the fur coat belonged to her mother, and I suspect the toque ornamented with peculiar feather bits did as well.

5   The groom is of an age and class where he could have owned his morning coat and striped trousers. They fit very well for hired ones. The suit is completely traditional down to the pearl-grey waistcoat (US vest) and carnation buttonhole.

6   The bride has a cream satin dress with a 'sweetheart' neckline, long tight sleeves, a full-flared and gathered skirt and the family veil held on by a pearl bead tiara.

A medley of international occasion wear

1   A tunic dress from the Sears Catalog 1947/8 decorated unnervingly with nail heads. The dress was made in the signature fabric of the forties, rayon crepe, in black of course, brown or dark moss green. Sears suggest it is an ideal frock for the fuller figure.

2   Luncheon dress by Digby Morton for Lachasse in navy and white check suiting. Designed in March 1947, it was destined to languish in the back of the wardrobe, overtaken by the New Look. If you could afford clothes like this you would naturally wear only the latest fashion.

3   The Hollywood version: the producer's wife at a première. This draped, sparkly dress was over a boned foundation and worn with a smart evening jacket made from Chinese silk brocade. The silver sandals and lots of jewelry complete the effect.

4   Seriously good taste from Balmain, who would have thought Mrs Producer vulgar. A beautifully fitted brocade jacket, mink trimmed, worn with a grand floor-sweeping satin skirt.

5   A bit of an oddity by Maggie Rouff for Miss Europe. Duchesse satin with beading and an unconvincing bustle. Mae West goes to Paris, perhaps?

1

2

3

4

5

Underwear and accessories

1 and 2   A spun-rayon nightdress and a classic wool flannel dressing gown (US robe) in women's sizes. The edges are neatly piped in a contrasting colour.

3   Bra and girdle made of rayon satin and marquisette with elastic panels.

4   Popular late-forties shoe – high heels, sling back, peep toe, platform sole. Assorted sensible colours and bow detail.

5   Sensible shoes of a shape that would continue to be manufactured for decades, ending up in extra wide fittings for the mature customers.

6   Modified wedgy sandal, for the summer.

7   One of an assortment of popular 'young' hat shapes with rolled brims – somewhat donut-like in shape.

8   Little boater.

9   A bonnet with rouleau trim.

10 and 11   Gloves, in leather or suede or cotton, were obligatory on most smart occasions. The classic handbag (purse) and a more adventurous bucket bag, were either in leather or, more frequently, in leatherette.

Leisure and sportswear

1   Playsuit. An open-necked shirt and neatly pressed tailored, flared shorts worn with wedgy espadrilles. Such simple open-air clothes were mostly American. English women were still deprived and rationed, so wasting precious coupons on new sports kit was not really an option.

2   Informal riding clothes – tweed hacking jacket, twill jodhpurs, brown leather jodhpur boots, soft shirt and tie. A felt hat or velvet cap could be worn for hacking, or a headscarf if preferred. These clothes were very well made in hard-wearing materials, so most English women would wear their pre-war kit and still look acceptably well turned out.

3   Sunsuit or swimsuit, a bra top with a tiny flared skirt over matching built-in knickers. Note the daringly bared midriff.

4   Tennis dress – in this instance a crisp white shirt tucked into a pair of white pleated shorts or a divided skirt. This style of garment became the standard girls' school games uniform; made in school colours of navy, maroon or brown and worn a regulation 15 cm (6 ins) above the knee, with an aertex shirt. The shorts were not at all flattering to the bulgier adolescent form and the aertex shirts shrank alarmingly, however huge they were to begin with.

5   Casual wear. A pair of rolled up blue denim jeans could be worn with a plaid lumberjack shirt or, as here, with a striped yachting jersey. Jeans did not become really popular in the UK until the sixties.

America versus England

1   English boys would have killed for such splendid clothes! Denim dungarees and an open-necked shirt, cotton or plaid, won hands down over grey shorts and school shirts. English parents, perhaps in revenge for the privations of rationing, seemed to delight in having their adolescent offspring look as unattractive as possible.

2   Hawaiian print sports shirt worn with woollen swimming trunks. Cotton boxer shorts rapidly became more popular, for obvious reasons. Note the belt, much needed if the weight of the wet wool was not to part the wearer from his swimsuit.

3   This is the sort of coordinated leisure wear that so horrified the English gent. 'Hollywood' tailored jacket in light wool, decorated with chocolate brown suede or Melton. A very bold tie and soft slacks completed the outfit.

4   The windcheater was a sort of early anorak made popular by President Eisenhower. Evolved from the battledress blouson jacket, it was much worn by golfers and film technicians as it was a comfortable alternative to the sports jacket, and was usually made in proofed cotton, or brown suede if you worked on the front end of a movie camera. Slacks, pullover shirts, hat and shoes came as standard.

5   English gentleman's athletic clothing. An old college blazer and cravat was probably the only strong colour permitted (for instance the shrimp pink worn by members of the Leander Rowing Club). These would be worn with a soft cream Viyella shirt and baggy shorts in khaki cotton. Smarter sporting events would warrant whites for tennis, or white flannel 'bags' – loosely cut trousers – for cricket and rowing.

6   The classic English city gent, emulated by solicitors and bank managers. Black bowler hat, three-piece dark suit or black jacket and waistcoat with pin-striped trousers, worn with a white or finely striped shirt with semi-stiff detachable collar, and a silk regimental or club tie in subdued colours. Black Oxford shoes and rolled umbrella complete the image.

7   The city gent off duty and the 'uniform' of the university-educated professional. A tweed sports jacket, its life extended by leather elbow patches, a soft-collared shirt often in a faint check, wool tie, trousers of grey flannel or cavalry twill, wool socks, laced brogues (usually of brown leather, sometimes

1   2   3   4

5   6   7

daringly of suede (known disparagingly as 'cad's creepers' or 'brothel creepers'). The outer garments were often made to measure for those who could afford it and, given the indestructible nature of the fabrics used, lasted for generations. Indeed the extreme age of a favourite sports coat was a source of subtle pride, especially since obvious newness was to be avoided lest the wearer be thought 'nouveau' or 'arriviste'.

Zooties

Zoot suits were an extraordinary expression of rebellion against the sober garments of the 1940s. They used yards of expensive, impractical fabric and were a defiantly ostentatious statement of cultural identity by the young black American male. They were also adopted by ambitious Mexican Americans. Unfortunately for this flamboyant, entertaining style, cloth rationing rendered such extravagance un-American, even illegal. Drunken, off-duty marines felt it their patriotic duty to attack Zoot suiters – beating them up and destroying their suits.

The style re-emerged in Colombia during the 1950s as a vigorous night club fashion, not unconnected with jazz and the consumption of marijuana.

The lady wears a halter-necked dance dress in white cloque.

CHAPTER 2

1950–55 – Paris rules

The 1950s are remembered as a time of renewal and of regained security. The shadow of the war was fading, rationing had come to an end, and the New Look heralded a decade of great vigour during which fashion was dominated by the great couturiers of Paris. Known only by their surnames, Dior, Balmain, Balenciaga, Givenchy ruled their salons, workrooms, clients and the fashion press with rigorous precision. Whims of iron indeed. Season by season the new styles appeared: the Princess line and the Tulip, the A-Line, the Trapeze, the Envol and the Sac. Each one became useless after its allotted season, to be superseded by the next.

This state of affairs was challenged from two angles: the first was the unstoppable rise of the working woman, the second was the new, alarming American phenomenon of the Teenager, for whom the essentially grown-up fashions of Paris were an irrelevance.

The ideal image of the decade was that of the family, which is hardly surprising when you consider the losses and upheavals of the war years. The typical fifties family, portrayed in countless magazines and advertisements, lived in a neat suburban house. Father, wearing a suit and a soft Trilby hat, left each morning to catch a commuter train to his place of employment where he spent the day earning his family's keep with other fathers, and flirting discreetly with his secretary. (We will come to her later.) Meanwhile, his pretty, cheerful wife took the two children to the local school, or sent them off with their packed lunch boxes to walk or cycle on their own, for the roads were safer then. She would then don an apron and rubber gloves and do the housework, making use of the many labour-saving devices now available. In the afternoon she might shop, cook or visit a similarly situated lady friend, always remembering to be home in time to make tea for the children, help with their homework and put them to bed before changing into an attractive dress in order to welcome her exhausted husband home from work with a cooling drink and a nice supper. At weekends her husband would wear his casual clothes and they would indulge in family outings to relations or places of interest.

Men and children had every interest in maintaining this idyll, but even at its height it was under threat because the children turned into teenagers and an increasing number of women refused to play the game.

This brings me to the secretary I mentioned earlier. An ever-increasing number of women worked as a matter of course before marriage, usually as typists, teachers or nurses. More women than ever went on to higher education and, with difficulty, forced themselves into medicine, the legal professions and even journalism, creating a demand for feminine business wear. Many saw no reason to lose their independence on marriage, and during this decade the harassed figure of the working mother appeared on the scene.

Men also began to be far more fashion-conscious. During the forties the ideal of the well-dressed gentleman was to look as inconspicuous as possible, an inclination encouraged by clothes rationing, when men had given their clothing coupons to their female relatives, so becoming shabbier than ever. The nostalgia that had prompted the New Look also affected men's fashions. The city gent began to borrow the styles of his Edwardian grandfather, complete with curly-brimmed bowler hat and navy single-breasted velvet-collared overcoat. It must have been a great surprise to these men that they were used as inspiration for the South London youths who became known as teddy boys. (Teds did not, however, wear bowler hats or carry rolled umbrellas.)

Young working women, though an unlikely counterpart to the vigorously working-class teddy boys, are at the other end of new young fashion. Both evolved ways of dressing that identified their class and chosen life style in a way that had only a little to do with the biannual changes of *haute couture*.

Designs from *Women & Beauty* 1950

The manufacturers of the garments drawn on this page have modified the extreme fashion statements of Dior and Balmain and created wearable classics that remained in fashion for many years.

1   'Little' tweed suit by Jaeger enlivened by red gloves and a matching silk scarf. Shoes and hat were brown. Then, as now, Jaeger clothes were known to be smart, well-made, well-designed and reassuringly unextreme. I have recently bought a nearly identical suit on sale as a current style.

2   Characteristic fifties dress for the home dressmaker, described thus: 'kimono-shaped bodice, the waist accentuated by patent leather belt; standout hip pockets on softly full skirt, big roll collar to give a deep neckline.' The dress is shown made up in deep red corduroy, khaki wool and dark green, trimmed with toning stripes.

3   Two-piece jersey jumper suit. This useful outfit has deep almost batwing sleeves and a straight skirt. It was made in two shades of green.

4   Flattering navy velour coat, with the hood lined in bright pink, by Windsmoor, another British firm still flourishing fifty years later.

5   An absolutely splendid swing-back coat in crimson wool. It has outsize pockets, collar and design features. This is another shape which comes back into fashion every five years or so.

1

2

3

4

5

Couture 1950–55

1   Batwinged peplum in pleated faille on a velvet, stem-skirted dress from the Hartnell collection of 1950. This interesting idea could be used to modernize last year's plain black evening dress, as the trained overskirt is easily detachable.

2   This cocktail dress is described as having a 'corolla bosom' – whatever that might be. The dress would be constructed on the stand by draping and folding stiffish satin or taffeta in the manner of an origami table napkin, and then stitching it to the rigidly boned and darted bodice. The double skirt, straight below, stiffened, flared with a dramatically asymmetric hem above, appeared in a collection by Jean Dessès.

3   'Shocking pink', the colour most closely identified with Elsa Schiaparelli (1890–1973), implies the combination of humour and outrageous elegance found in this designer's imaginative work. The pink overskirt and bodice is embroidered with tiny jet beads in a striking baroque pattern, by the long-established firm of Lesage. The crinoline-shaped underskirt is black silk organza over a stiffened petticoat.

4   The American designer Charles James (1906–78) was described by Balenciaga as having raised dressmaking from 'an applied art to a pure art form'. He built his clothes like architecture, over a complex substructure more usually associated with sculptural engineering than fashion. James called this dress 'four-leaved clover' and made it from the heaviest quality ivory silk duchesse satin (which would cost about £80 ($120) per metre these days if you could still get it) inset with perfect black velvet.

5   Men's evening clothes did not change much in the early 1950s. Older men still wore dinner jackets and, for grand occasions, tails with a white tie, that had no doubt been made for them before the war. Very young men quite often wore their father's suits. However, the upper and upper-middle classes still regularly changed for dinner at least on special occasions, so the possession of a black dinner jacket, either single- or double-breasted, was still a normal part of a gentleman's wardrobe.

1

2

3

4

5

Parisian couture in the fifties

1 Fifties chic by Balmain. Princess line wool dress with bias-cut crepe neck and short sleeves. Swathed drum hat, long gloves, lots of pearls.

2 Glamour by Balenciaga. Dinner suit in black velvet and moiré with an out-size collar and witty hat. The tiny pillbox, in this case with a stiffened tassel sticking out behind, was typical Balenciaga and beautifully balances the exotic proportions of the suit.

3 Also by Balmain, for his younger customers. Dresses such as this, made as here in lace and tulle or frequently in satin and poult with net underskirts, swirled through countless balls and dances. Note that the solid heels of the early 1950s are now lethal stiletto points.

4 This was thought to be the acceptable way to smoke – head thrown back and with a long cigarette holder. This is Dior 1950 with a very smart re-working of the artist's smock into a hugely bloused top, with a very tight skirt.

5 *En vol* double apron day dress by Dior in fine check tweed with a velvet Peter Pan collar and bias-cut cuffs. This charmingly silly idea could well have been the forerunner of Vivienne Westwood's padded bottoms four decades later, designed rather more for the photographers than the public.

1

2

3

4

5

ST. HILDA'S C.E. HIGH SCHOOL
Croxteth Drive, Sefton Park
LIVERPOOL
L17 3AL
Founded 1894
A Grant Maintained School

Bohemia

1   This over-size sweater – known as the Sloppy Joe – was hated by middle-class parents, and therefore became a modest symbol of rebellion. Here worn by a young actress, hair cropped ready to be asked to play Joan of Arc, and teamed with tight ski pants and ballet pumps. This look became a favourite with art students and indeed most girls with creative ambitions.

2   The successful poet. Odd and baggy Irish tweed coat worn over a surprisingly well-pressed check suit and cheery bow tie. The umbrella is not tightly furled.

3   Black polo neck jumper worn with flannel or tweed slacks, much favoured by conductors and actors when rehearsing.

4   A very grand film director slumming it. Crumpled Italian suit worn with a knitted sports shirt and the obligatory cigarette.

5   Actresses led the way in reintroducing the raincoat as a glamorous garment. This example has storm flaps and is in plastic-coated cotton. They did look very good, and their cheapness made them very popular: art students and prostitutes favoured black, to the confusion of kerb-crawlers.

1

2

3

4

5

Men's outer wear

1   The new formality. City coat in Crombie wool with black velvet collar. A tight descendant of the Edwardian frock coat, worn over formal black jacket and pin-stripe trousers, bowler hat and the rest.

2   Successful composer. Pre-war double-breasted suit and a rather theatrical cloak.

3   Biker. When Marlon Brando starred in *On the Waterfront* wearing a Perfecto leather jacket and denim jeans, whole platoons of teenagers yearned for a jacket like his. It was based on a flying jacket, and became the essential garment not only for bikers, but for rock stars and the seriously butch of both sexes. It is worn with a tight T-shirt and tighter jeans. The six-segment cap, padded gloves and heavy boots are also leather. As a 'look' it has proved astonishingly enduring; only the other day I encountered in my village an entire family, including grandparents, so attired, resting beside their machines. The look sprang up, apparently fully formed, as early as 1954.

1

2

3

Four generations of a middle-class English family

1   Grandmother. Her coat is of the then fashionable pony skin, trimmed and collared with beaver. It seems that every woman apart from the very poor owned at least one fur coat. They were a desirable status symbol, but with efficient central heating still an unusual luxury in the home, and almost unheard of in popular cars, they also helped to solve the problem of keeping both warm and smart.

2   The small boy wears a traditional tweed coat with matching cap, and gaiters – an infuriating garment with a huge number of fiddly buttons and a strap under the foot. They were worn by boys and girls since long trousers or warm tights were either considered unsuitable or were not available.

3   The boy's mother wears her good suit – nearly New Look, with a neat waist and double pocket detail and a fullish pleated skirt, worn with well-polished shoes.

4   Great-grandmother is not wearing her fur coat for once, replacing it with a smart edge-to-edge swing-back cloth coat. Like Queen Mary, the elderly often wore ankle-length skirts left over from the thirties, or even earlier, never having adopted the short skirts of the forties (or twenties). Her flowerpot hat is trimmed with flowers in dark silk.

5   Maternity clothes remained quite a problem, since decorum still demanded that you conceal the bulge for as long as possible. This young mother-to-be wears a simple smock top and wrap-around skirt.

1

2

3

4

5

Young actresses photographed in 1955 by Norman Parkinson

1   The most conventional of the three wears a neat check wool pinafore dress and almost sensible shoes. She wears her dress with a polo neck jumper – had she been a secretary the jumper would probably have been a crisp white shirt-blouse.

2   Corduroy smock and knickerbocker suit. This is something of an original, as breeches were not usually worn in a non-sporting situation. However they are a sensible solution to rehearsals. She wears ballet pumps and seamed stockings.

3   A more American look with the girl's hair in a ponytail; she wears her polo neck jumper tucked into high-waisted tartan ski pants and curious laced dance pumps.

4   The black leotard top is worn with a long circular skirt and stole in enormous checks. This dramatic outfit was an excellent solution to informal dinner parties in draughty country houses, being warm and attractive and allowing you to keep your vest on.

1

2

3

4

Hair

1, 2 and 3   In the fifties it was usual to wash and style hair at home, but chemical permanent-waving solutions were sufficiently dangerous and unpredictable to send most women to the increasing band of professional hairdressers. These three examples of 'Salon Perm' advertisements demonstrate the decade's obsession with rigid personal grooming. Typically the hair would be cut and permed every six or seven weeks, and once a week, or once a fortnight if money was a bit short, the hair would be washed and set, again by the hairdresser. Even schoolgirls slept in wire and coin rollers, kept in place by hairnets or silk scarves. The tortured hairstyles now only seen in ballroom dancing competitions stem from this period.

4   Boys and men went to the barber once a month and had a 'short back & sides, please' without the option. Long hair was considered frighteningly decadent and unmanly. Almost no one rebelled.

5   The alternative. When my mother allowed me to have an urchin cut in 1953 she was thought to be encouraging a dangerously arty and independent streak, in the small provincial town where I grew up. The freedom from hair grips and slippery hair ribbons was splendid.

6   Girls often pushed their shoulder-length hair back under a velvet band, made with a bit of elastic at the back to ensure a snug fit. In the late fifties and early sixties this would be substituted by a folded scarf.

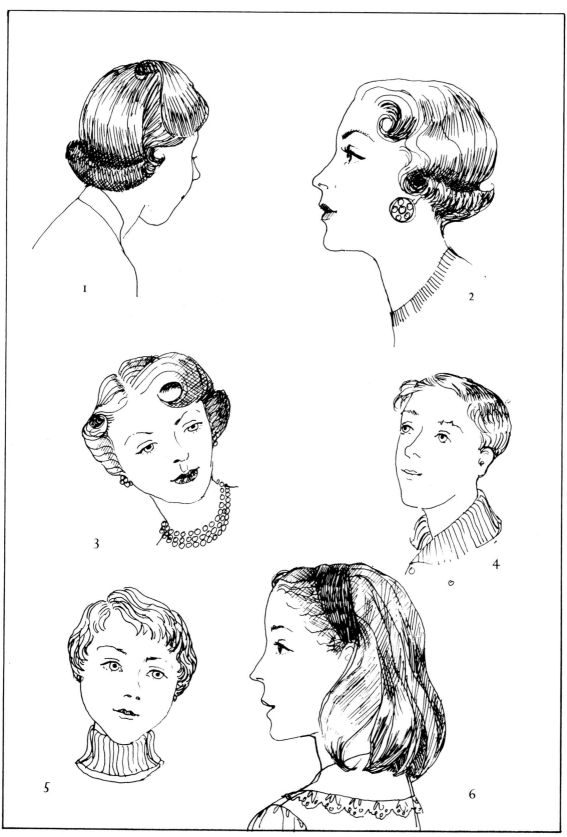

CHAPTER 3

1955–60 – The rise of the teenager

Before 1950 children became girls or youths at around the age of puberty, and at about eighteen years of age they became adults. They had no special styles and no spending power. By the end of the decade things were very different. Many young people in their late teens had some kind of paid work, which, as long as you were not having to pay much rent, you could actually live on. The young, armed with this new spending power, demanded their own fashions, their own places of entertainment where they could listen to their own music.

By the mid-fifties there were clubs where students in over-sized sweaters jived to the new rock 'n' roll bands and dance halls where skiffle groups played Bill Haley's 'Rock Around the Clock'. Leather boys in jeans and black, many-zippered jackets, fed juke boxes in coffee bars, and all day the new Italian machines made coffee in espresso bars, milk bars, soda fountains, Wimpys and ice cream parlours. It was all very noisy but, to look back on, curiously innocent. Except among the fast and decadent jazz musicians themselves, drugs were still substances you were given by the doctor when you were unwell; gay still meant happy and nice girls didn't go all the way.

The clothes worn by the young were largely defined by the boys, in itself a new trend. Girls' clothes were fairly restrained; they might wear a buttoned cardigan with a string of beads and a simple skirt or pinafore dress or, more daringly, tight trousers and ballet shoes – it was considered tarty to wear high heels with trousers. In summer a full cotton skirt was worn over several layers of crackling petticoats (my school tried to ban them), with flesh-coloured stockings and stiletto heels.

Boys, other than American preppies or the English public school product, could choose from short Italian jackets, fluorescent socks, winkle-picker shoes, leather jackets and jeans or a shaggy sweater and sandals.

It was a reversal of *Vogue*'s world where fashion could begin only in Paris and then filter down to the street. Now teenage fashions began in the city streets and worked their way outwards and upwards. In 1959 the all-powerful fashion journalists began to notice that their domain was beginning to show signs of insubordination and started to question the new trends. 'What does fashion represent?' *Vogue* asked. 'Decoration, disguise, a mood of society. For millions of working teenagers clothes are the biggest pastime in life, a symbol of independence and the fraternity of an age group. The origin of the teenage look might be urban and working class, but it has been taken up with alacrity by the King's Road. It owes nothing to Paris or Savile Row; something to entertainment idols (the Tommy Steele haircut ... the Bardot sex babe look) and much to Italy.'

In 1955 a new art-school-trained British designer called Mary Quant opened a shop called Bazaar in the King's Road, Chelsea, to sell the artlessly simple clothes that by the next decade would make her the major fashion force in the world outside Paris. Her shop became the social centre for the bohemian Chelsea Set, and soon the new-style café society was blooming in little French and Italian bistros and the latest help-yourself boutiques began to overrun the grocery shops and artists' pubs that had originally lined the King's Road.

The gossip columns now began to be dominated by this Chelsea Set, who liked to fraternize with the left-wing playwrights and actors of the English Stage Company at the Royal Court Theatre, handily situated in Sloane Square at the western end of the King's Road. This theatre company has been credited with the single-handed revival of the British theatre, replacing West End drawing room comedies with gritty dramas involving angry young men and kitchen sinks. John Osborne's play *Look Back in Anger*, staged to exceedingly mixed critical reviews in 1965, was a liberating attack on patrician complacency or one long whinge, depending on your stance.

In America, the ultimate bohemians were the Beats; a generation of college drop-outs who could be found leading nomadic and amoral lives from Berkeley, California to Greenwich Village in New York. They discovered marijuana, published poetry and read the novels of Jack Kerouac. In London, their influence gradually overcame the working-class primness of the Royal Court set during the next decade.

Fashion details

1 'Glamorize your beauty zone' says the advertisement for this well-cut strapless bra. The pernicious skeletal ideal may already have gripped *haute couture* in its deadly clutches, but real women needed seriously well-engineered help, and the new nylon fabrics and elasticized satins were perfect for the job.

2 Smart quiffed hair-cut, long, greasy and hated by the middle classes.

3 Crocodile winkle-picker shoe to wear with the above hair-do.

4 Impossibly rigid standards of grooming, as promoted by women's magazines at this time, intimidated all but the most rigorous of fashion's followers. This model has it all: cast iron rollered hair-do, perfect make-up with the ubiquitous cat's-eye liner in stark black and dark lipstick with matching nail varnish, and sparkly modern jewelry. Boned corsetry made sure that no unseemly slouching occurred. Women looked fifteen years younger the minute this look loosened up in the sixties.

5 Diamanté bows decorate the shoulders of this poult evening dress.

6 Resort fashion. Sun hat to protect the frizzled perm, dark glasses, cigarette holder and lipstick as in town.

7 Stately swimsuit in french navy with white lace-covered insert. The rubber swimming cap was obligatory for lady swimmers – it did protect the hair-do, but not even little rubber petals could make the things flattering.

Claire McCardell and the teenager

1   Co-ed student at Syracuse University – 1955. Peter-Pan-collared blouse, cardigan, tweed skirt, bobby-sox and loafers; all prepared for a good marriage to the man in the grey flannel suit.

2   Late fifties' sack dress, stretched taut over the lady's rear.

3   This little dress looks both back to the New Look and forward to the sixties' mini-skirt. It is difficult to divine the occasion it was designed for – the original photograph shows a department store carrier bag, but it does look overdressed for just shopping.

4 and 5   Two innovative designs by the wonderful Claire McCardell, who really invented American fashion! The denim summer dress on the left is apparently just two huge triangles of fabric held by a slim belt. Miss McCardell was the first to use dance clothes for street wear, using leotards as a 'body' with matching tights; the striped wrap skirt and ballet pumps make a versatile and useful look. Her clothes are nearly impossible to date, and the American design industry owes her an enormous debt.

1

2

3

4

5

Dior, Jacques Griffe and Marion

The three couture outfits on this page are high fashion, indicative of the almost tyrannical hold that each new season's 'lines' had on clothes. Marion's summery offering (*below, left*) was far more likely to be what most women actually wore.

1   Smart day suit in fine black wool, belted on the natural waistline, Dior 1957.

2   Trapeze dress by Dior. You can often tell if a garment is *haute couture* because the waist is in the wrong place, or in this case non-existent. Dior would not have been amused when this shape was enthusiastically adopted by the pregnant, the waistless and the frankly stout. The model's rather twee pose reminds us that this is fashion, but not for long.

3   Day dress by Marion in striped pure cotton with a stiff collar, wide belt and five widths of fabric box-pleated into the naturally placed trim waist. (It would have to be trim, with those horizontal stripes.) Layers of sugar-washed nylon frills give the skirt its bounce.

4   This neo-twenties hobbled day dress by Jacques Griffe was also destined for the sale rail. It is a truism that if a woman has a waist she prefers to show it, and if she has not she has no wish to pay designer prices to hide it.

1

2

3

4

Maternity

It is no accident that we had to wait until the late fifties for pregnancy to become fashionable. Immediately after the war came a tremendous 'baby boom' which lasted for ten years or so. The reasons for this are too obvious to need explaining here. But as it became desirable to produce healthy babies to compensate for the loss of so many of their potential fathers, so women were encouraged to feel pride in their condition rather than just putting up with it. These examples are all from a smart Italian magazine called *Cosi* and were possibly the first suggestion that it is possible to be pregnant and (fairly) stylish.

1   This two-piece with a jaunty tie neck made in grey shantung became a classic shape.

2 and 3   Two pretty pleated smock tops, which retain the crisp neat details of the period.

4   Sun-dress in navy polka dot cotton. A circle of fabric is attached to the white piqué yoke – a simple and attractive solution!

5   This is a very elegant designer dress with a sunray-pleated front and a large bow at the neck which was thought to distract the eye from the bulge.

6   The idea that a very pregnant woman could indulge in the pleasures of sea bathing would have seemed outrageous to the older generation. This crossover from romper style swimsuit solves the problem splendidly. Note the obligatory rubber cap with little fins on – I think they're supposed to be leaves.

1

2

3

4

5

6

1950s Girls

1 and 2   Summer dresses in washable cottons were a warm weather uniform for little girls, and were the basics for school uniforms for many years. Such dresses were surprisingly well made; matching knickers, three-inch hems and generous turnings in the side seams were standard practise, so that a favourite dress would be handed down to younger sisters or cousins.

3   Sunsuit in washable cotton. A comfortable playsuit for the very young, to be worn with a cotton sun hat and bucket and spade.

4   Sun-dress. A term applied to any simple cotton dress that exposed the shoulders and upper back. This classic shape is still worn, if not in fashion, to this day.

5   Hand-smocked dress and knickers for a toddler. These pretty babies' garments were often made at home, by a skilled mother or grandmother out of 'Liberty lawn', a very fine cotton usually with a small all-over flower print, and painstakingly embroidered across the yoke and chest. They were so well made that they could often be handed on to the next generation.

6   Shorts and neat top. A tomboyish alternative to the tennis frock, or skirt.

1

2

3

4

5

6

English uniforms

1 and 2   Girls' school. Insisting that adolescents wear middle-aged hairstyles and unflattering uniforms was a peculiarly British phenomenon. All schools except for a few 'progressive' establishments did insist until quite recently, and a few still do, on the grounds that it promoted team spirit and cooperation. It is certainly easier as a parent to know that your increasingly independent offspring has no choice in the matter. On the whole girls' uniforms were as similar as possible to their brothers', simply substituting a gored or pleated skirt for grey flannel trousers (2). In summer, however, simple shirt-waist dresses were worn, often with white collars, in a range of striped or checked cotton, with a cardigan in the school colour against the chill (1). For colder weather, the school blazer was worn with a shirt and tie, and a cardigan or V-neck sweater was added for warmth. Some schools still wore soft grey or navy felt hats, with straw boaters in summer, but a beret became an attractive alternative. Fee-paying schools added smart Harris tweed coats, belted raincoats and occasionally a skirt suit; as well as the clothing needed for a variety of team games, usually lacrosse or hockey, and netball, an English forerunner of basketball.

3   The smarter boys' schools expected their students to look like trainee bank managers. For classroom and formal wear black jackets with the school crest were worn with a waistcoat (vest), or V-neck sweater, striped black and grey or plain grey trousers. Really grand schools still insisted on stiff white collars, with studs, and a boater.

4   Not strictly a uniform, but close. The duffle-coat was designed for naval officers to wear to sea, so it was quite natural for it to be adopted by other professional men who had to stand around in the cold encouraging other chaps to run about. Here the coat is worn over a variety of checks – checkered flat cap – shirt and tie – discreetly checkered tweed sports jacket. The trousers were probably in a plain fabric.

5   Roger Bannister, the first man to run a mile in four minutes in 1955, achieved his record in a singlet made of cotton jersey with the logo of the Amateur Athletics Association on the chest, his number card safely pinned on, front and back, cotton drill elastic-waisted shorts and black spiked running shoes. No Lycra anywhere.

1

2

3

4

5

Teds and others

1   San Francisco bohemian from *The Subterraneans*, a film loosely based on Jack Kerouac's novel. This was the relatively staid beginning of the Beat Generation. The dancer wears very tight black ski pants and a black striped top with fairly tidy Bardot-esque hair and a lot of eye makeup.

2   The Teddy Boy, or Ted was an accidental by-product of the tailors of Savile Row. The flamboyant frock-coat-length jacket, brocade waistcoat and narrow trousers was aimed at their usual upper-class customers, the majority of whom were far too conservative to adopt it. However, the idea of dressing in a way that ridiculed 'toffs' and also looked exotic and glamorous touched a loud chord in the young urban working-class male. Details were added: narrow cowboy tie, zootie styling, suede shoes with immensely thick crepe soles known as 'brothel creepers'. The Ted attracted a great deal of horrified media attention and confirmed everyone's worst suspicions by acting the part of hooligan, slashing cinema seats and flashing flick-knives and greasy combs, so that the term 'Teddy Boy' became interchangeable with 'delinquent'. Compared to the later teen tribes such as Hell's Angels, punks and skinheads, the Ted is now remembered almost with affection.

3   The folky precursor of grunge, born-again Christians and the Liberal Party. Ted Polhemus defines folkies as a distinctive group – young people who aspired to a purer, rural, more hand-crafted aesthetic. He makes distinction between the nihilism of the beatniks who despaired of humanity, and the optimism of 'the folkies who felt that given the chance, and the right music, something could be done'. The tendency to political activism has convinced many that it is not possible to be left-wing and well dressed, though the activists would say that they had more important issues to think about than matching accessories.

4   The intellectual. This lady's feelings about clothes were mostly negative. She did not want to appear prim, bourgeois, dainty or sweet, or any of the things that the bossier glossies would have her be. This made the choice of suitable clothes surprisingly difficult; increasingly the solution was to wear black, and borrow your boy-friend's coat and, in this case, college scarf.

5   The early rock singer was not an intellectual, even if his shirt owes something to the American folk singer. He wears an open-necked piped shirt, tight pants, and slightly too much jewelry.

Newsreel

1   By 1956 Elvis Presley, former truck driver from the deep south and the undisputed King of Rock 'n' Roll, had made three influential movies – *Heartbreak Hotel*, *Hound Dog* and *Love me Tender*. It has been said that without him modern pop music might not have happened, or at least would have taken a different form. The vocal style that he made his own was lifted straight from the Black popular music of the period, then filtered through both Gospel singing and Country and Western music. The connections between the style of music and the apparel of the musician are endlessly fascinating; never more so than in the case of 'Elvis the Pelvis'! He influenced two style tribes, firstly the working cowboy look which reached its apogee with Ralph Lauren two decades later, and secondly by wearing ever more outrageous stage costumes that made him the original Rhinestone Cowboy and spawned a generation of imitators.

In 1958 Elvis was drafted into the US Army to the accompaniment of intense media attention, and served in Germany for eighteen months. It must have been an interesting experience for both parties.

2   Ralph Vaughan Williams was the grand old man of English music till his death in 1958. He was not interested in fashion. The baggy grey suit could have been anything up to twenty years old, and his daily wear of a grey knitted waistcoat, soft shirt and well-worn tie were typical of his class and profession.

3   This is a sketch of the great Miles Davis, exponent of cool jazz and hero of many a student at the time. I checked the date of this photograph several times, as the long lurex overshirt comes as a great surprise. It is another example of where black American musicians go, everyone else goes sooner or later.

4   In 1957 Pulitzer-prize-winning playwright Arthur Miller married film-star and sex symbol Marilyn Monroe. This American intellectual wears a pale summer-weight three-button jacket, dark tie and pleat front trousers.

5   Either this English painter was very poor, or his mind was far above clothes; I think he has tried to mend the pocket of his old tweed coat himself with string, and although he was very popular as a painter of vigorous, somewhat orange portraits his reclusive nature did not allow for much in the way of coordinated leisure wear.

Balmain and others

1   Balmain's design credo was that dressmaking is the architecture of movement. At the height of his fame he designed exquisite clothes for royalty, movie-stars, glamorous ladies of – as the French put it – 'a certain age', actresses in plays and films, as well as air-hostess uniforms and, most surprising of all, roomy garments for Gertrude Stein and Alice B Toklas.

This sketch shows a matching outfit of a relaxed coat worn over a fine wool suit, with a spotted neckscarf in the same silk as the coat lining.

2   A remarkable evening dress made from a half-circle of silk printed in a bold abstract design and constructed with a single seam. It is an oddity well out of the main stream but an interesting experiment nonetheless.

3   This dress in cornflower blue georgette over blue taffeta was made for Princess Alexandra. The simple transparent bodice is mounted on a boned bustier; and the straight cocktail-length skirt is draped in the same georgette. She wore it in a series of photographs by the English photographer and designer Cecil Beaton.

1

2

3

CHAPTER 4

1960–65 – The Kennedy years

If the late 1950s were a time of hope, the early sixties seemed, at least for the young, to be years when much that was hoped for had been achieved. The youth of America and Europe were more than fashionable, they *were* fashion. The permissive society got under way accompanied by the haunting tones of four boys from Liverpool who became the most popular human beings on the planet: the Beatles. Sexual and social taboos were eroded, changes epitomized by hallucinogenic drugs, the contraceptive pill and the mini-skirt. As is often the case, short skirts and frantic social change were the visible froth on the groundswell of much greater turbulence. The British Prime Minister, Harold Macmillan, made a famous speech about the 'wind of change' blowing through Africa as Britain, France and Belgium released country after country to the unstoppable tide of black nationalism. In the United States black civil rights leader Martin Luther King fought for recognition against the forces of prejudice and inertia and, despite ugly outbreaks of white supremacist viciousness, he achieved more in a few years than had been managed for a generation.

Meanwhile, the Cold War between the superpowers of the United States and the Soviet Union rumbled on, bringing the world as close as it has ever been to nuclear war.

The decade began with spectacular scientific and medical achievements. Russia and America spent billions of dollars to prove their supremacy in space with rockets, sputniks and eventually manned spacecraft. The first human heart transplant promised, for a while, to conquer death itself until America's young President Kennedy was shot in the head by Lee Harvey Oswald in Dallas, Texas in 1963.

The new social order was unrecognizable, uncongenial and deeply alarming to members of the old establishment. For a while the traditional events of society and the summer Season seemed likely to be swept away by the egalitarian tide, for in the sixties only the young were news. There was a new élite in the West, its members were all young and all concerned with the creation of image; photographers and hairdressers, pop singers, actors, models, interior decorators, writers and designers. They came from all kinds of backgrounds; from London's East End to America's wealthy East Coast. Because their prestige was

1. VE Day 1945. Women and children in England at the end of World War II in Europe

3. Evening dress in sunray pleats *1955*

4. His and her pinstripes 1960

5. Girl in a red and white striped cotton dress, with two boys in the background, summer 1961

6. Op art suit illustrated in *Vogue* 1965

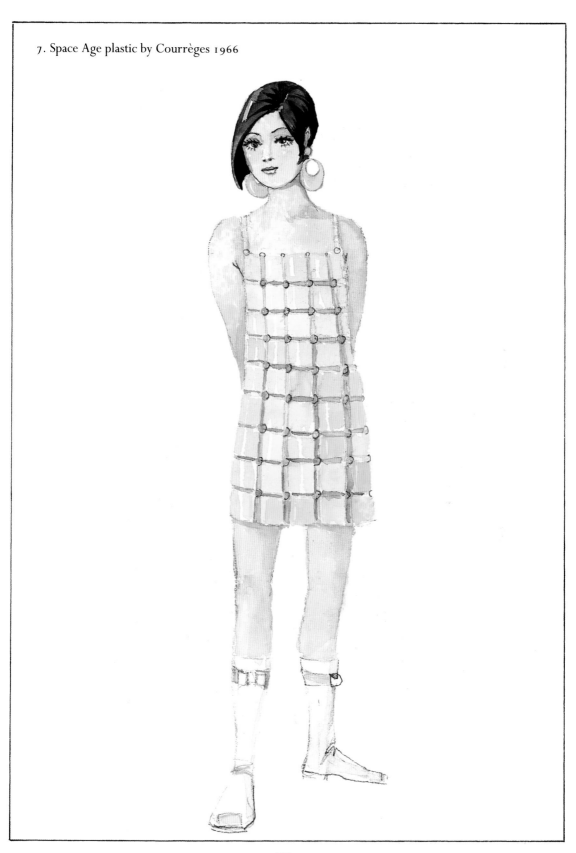

8. Three hippies from Hyde Park 1968

founded on talent rather than inherited wealth they shared a great respect for professionalism and held the old-fashioned amateur in contempt. The cult of the working-class hero meant that, in bohemian circles, if you spoke with an upper-class accent you took some pains to disguise it and if your politics tended to the right you kept quiet about it.

Fashion reflected the interest in the Space Age by incorporating new man-made fabrics in stark geometric shapes. Two important designers of the decade were Paco Rabane and Courrèges (see page 92). Rabane made chain-mail dresses from lightweight plastic paillettes, to be worn with huge plastic ear-rings and rings made from Perspex. Silver or chrome became the precious metal of choice and white a major couture colour. The favourite dress was a brief sleeveless shift worn with a short sharp haircut and false eyelashes.

The extent of the fashion revolution could instantly be seen in men's clothes. Longer hair, printed shirts, no ties and skin-tight jeans became commonplace. Homosexuality at last ceased to be a criminal offence and, as the newly-legal gay men in the creative professions stepped gingerly out of the closet, they quickly raised the standards of male elegance now that they no longer had to disguise themselves as straight.

The attitude held by ordinary Englishmen, that an interest in sartorial display or excessive personal hygiene was effete or worse, was still firmly in place in politics, the city and the armed forces. But liberation in the arts began to infiltrate even these bastions of tradition.

'Running away from the grey pox', *Vogue* explained, was a recurring theme of the decade and a brittle newness for its own sake became the admired quality. It talked of a lust for professionalism, but in fact the visual arts were in some confusion. Figurative painting underpinned by academic life drawing was suddenly completely unacceptable, as was harmony in modern music. As a result, students of fine art were not taught to draw in case it damaged their natural talent. Abstract painting and a-tonal music were the only acceptable forms of expression in serious art circles, and if your talent was representational then you had better use it in one of the many applied design fields such as stage design, graphic art, advertising or textile design; and if your musical ability involved the composition of tunes, then you turned to the theatre, films or TV for employment. You might not be accepted as a 'serious' artist, but at least it was possible to earn a living by your creative talents without selling out to commerce.

Children

1   Little girls now get their own fashionable look. This is a smart, if somewhat scratchy, 'shift' in black and white striped washable Welsh wool. The simple shape remained a classic, although with the development of man-made, drip-dry fabrics it became increasingly unusual to make children's dresses in wool.

2   A boy with his first 'man's' haircut, in the same issue of *Vanity Fair*, September 1964. He is wearing an unstructured wool blazer and grey marl shorts. All boys and girls seem to have worn short white socks while very young, followed by knee-length socks held up by garters of varying efficiency.

3   A Cub, the junior version of the Boy Scout. This worldwide boys' movement was founded in 1908 by Lord Baden-Powell, whose lively concern with adolescents in short trousers might be regarded with extreme suspicion today. The green sweater and khaki shorts were a version of the standard boy's uniform and if it reminds us of the Hitler Youth, this was certainly never remarked upon at the time.

4   Pinafore rompers for a toddler to wear over a blouse or jersey. The toddler, like the teenager, was a new age-group eagerly welcomed by marketing personnel. Even so, rompers were an excellent invention as they fitted neatly over saggy terry nappies.

5   This pretty sun-dress from a 1960 *Vogue* has a gingham skirt attached to a white cotton bodice decorated with appliquéd tulips. It could well have been made from a paper pattern, with the flowers lovingly stitched on by the child's mother. The child has been allowed to remove her socks, a real sign of high summer.

6   Long dresses for children remained popular for bridesmaids, often matching the bride's older attendants in fabric, if not in cut. This simple dress with a raised waist is made interesting by the use of broderie anglaise and a coloured sash.

7   Home dressmaking was very popular, with a multitude of excellent paper patterns for the amateur, ranging from this easy two-piece pinafore dress, to the most challenging couture outfits. Versions of this useful style were made in all sorts of fabrics and worn with any blouse or polo neck already in the wardrobe.

1

2

3

4

5

6

7

Underwear

1   In the 1960s almost all women wore some sort of foundation garment as well as a bra. They were available in all sorts of styles. Sarong girdles (as here), pull-on and panty-girdles, long-line corselettes, all-in-ones – ranging from industrial-strength near-corsets involving pink rubber and circle-stitched cotton, to airy confections of Spandex, nylon and lace. This firm Berlei bra and girdle featured a cross-over front, effective as a vigorous tummy flattener, and an efficient, if rather pointed, bra.

2   A bra and pull-on girdle aimed at the younger market, described as 'on the go casuals with the fabulous Gossard lift'. Breasts were worn a couple of inches higher than nature intended and never allowed to wobble.

3   This is the 'co-star', designed, the ad says 'to mould you to woman's most envied shape. The wonderful star-formed cups to make *more* of the wonderful figure that is yours in only co-star'. I remember hating the torpedo breasts this type of bra produced and spent quite a lot of time stitching across the points to produce a rounder shape.

4   While English women had to put up with boring underwear in white or Germoline pink, their American sisters could have pretty coloured prints, such as the bra and long panty girdle shown here that was available in Spanish Sherry, Granada Pink or Madrid Blue. You could even buy D and E cups in attractive colours, whereas the average English store only stocked large sizes in nursing-mother styles in boilable white cotton.

5   The Baby Doll nightie set, so-called after Caroll Baker wore such a garment throughout the film *Baby Doll*. Normally made in nylon and trimmed with nylon lace, and sporting matching knickers, it was thought to be the last word in provocative dressing – despite a tendency to be sticky and uncomfortable. Sets like this are still available, though usually in red or black see-through nylon and only in sex shops.

1

2

3

4

5

Parkinson's page

1   The great Norman Parkinson photographed the models on this page for *Queen* Magazine. Possibly the only photographer who combined glamour with an enchanting sense of the absurd, his pictures define the look of any period in which he worked. This coat made from Aztec-inspired wool blanket is a typical choice. The straight, simple shape, waist-length sleeves and hem exactly on the knee are synonymous with the more ladylike aspects of the sixties but the bohemian fabric lifts the whole image from ordinariness.

2   Weeks of work must have gone into this grand evening two-piece. The knee-length silk tunic is encrusted with beads worked in a daisy-like design, each flower spilling over with dangling crystal bugle beads. The motifs on the underskirt (which I suspect has a simple camisole top) are simpler, though the beads on the hem must have come adrift at the first dance.

3   One of three little black dresses from the Paris collections of 1961. It was worn with a boned backless and strapless bra, hardly necessary on the skinny model but crucial on those better endowed. The sombre black is enlivened by the silly pink cocktail hat of ruched silk organza.

1

2

3

Sportswear

1   Skiing became increasingly fashionable and, with the proliferation of package tour companies offering all-in deals of comparative cheapness and chummy efficiency, the winter holiday was within the reach of many people for the first time. Department stores from Macy's to Lillywhites catered for growing interest in this sport. This girl is wearing a kagool or anorak in waterproofed poplin; the cheerful check is reversible to plain blue or red and is worn with stretch pants reinforced with bri-nylon. The stitched centre-front crease and strap under the foot kept the look neat. Ski pants, usually in black, became the uniform of the female art student, before being overtaken by jeans.

2   Tennis dress by Teddy Tinling. Even quite informal play demanded whites. Discreet coloured trim was allowed, on buttons and piping to begin with but becoming increasingly bolder as fashions changed. This smartly tailored dress has a picture collar buttoning into a small waist belt. All sorts of shirt-and-skirt or shirt-and-shorts ensembles were also acceptable.

3   The tennis professional wears long white trousers, and a windcheater when not actually playing. Men still wore long trousers, as they continue to do for cricket, but increasingly white shorts replaced them.

4   A casual ensemble, of a printed silk or rayon shirt-blouse worn tucked into a cummerbund, if you had the waist, or outside the tight three-quarter-length pants, if you didn't. Considering the level of the girl's grooming, which includes roller waved hair and full makeup, the bare feet and flip-flops come as a bit of a surprise. Stockings or, from the middle of the decade, tights were worn on all formal occasions and always in 'town', however hot the weather.

5   Even nice girls take to wearing bikinis. This one in gingham is trimmed with broderie anglaise and has a matching sun hat.

6   One-piece cotton playsuit, with a lightly boned strapless top and side-zippered shorts. The brightly patterned drawstring skirt is made of fine terry towelling and could be pulled flat to use for drying, sitting upon and as a sort of impromptu changing tent for the beach.

Early sixties man

1   Narrow-cut suit in pretend-mohair with Terylene, one of the new man-made yarns that made lightweight fabrics as easy-care as the new drip-dry shirts. The new young styles were originated by Italian tailors but quickly caught on in both England and America. Such a flashy look never gained the approval of Old Money or the aristocracy but the increasing power of youth hardly cared about that. Tight trousers were worn over winkle-picker shoes, with button-down shirts and long string ties.

2   The car coat became associated with used-car salesmen and all that was slightly 'dodgy' about the post-war era. Car ownership increased so dramatically in the sixties that it is not surprising that a whole culture was devoted to it. The little curly trilby and leather driving gloves completed this long-lasting look, more long-lasting than the fake fur collar on the coat.

3   Glasgow market. This image of the working-class man is a good illustration of how smart middle-class styles become the workwear of the next generation. The wide-lapelled jacket looks like a demob suit to me and the Fair Isle sweater, that would once have been worn by fashionable golfers, is now worn instead of a waistcoat (vest) on the cold Glasgow streets.

4   Winkle-picker shoe in fine Italian leather, with hand-tooled detail.

5   The half-wellington, Chelsea, spring-sided or elastic-sided boot. A smart boot of military origin, much liked by officers and gentlemen because of the un-interrupted line formed by the plain front under the cuff-less trouser.

6   Casual suede shoes, still being sold in cut-price catalogues in the nineties.

Women's coats

1   There were many experiments in man-made fabrics. Foam-back coating was not too successful. It was rather like a rubber wetsuit, stiff and sweaty, though not too unpleasant until the glue bonding the foam to the cloth began to degrade.

2 and 3   Classic wool suits inspired by Paris. The collar set away from the neck is typical. The jacket relies on a skilful shaping of the side-body seams and three-quarter length sleeves. The bust dart springing from a side-body seam in (3) became a signature of the period, especially used by Biba a decade later. Both the straw sailor boater and the round furry cloche hat were popular shapes and gloves were still compulsory on even semi-formal occasions.

4   An oddity that became a classic: the three-quarter-length fake fur casual coat, worn with a fine black wool jumper and tight ski pants. No one minded very much about either the ozone layer or the fate of small furry animals in the sixties but, even so, fake fur became acceptable, as it was cheap and 'amusing'.

5   A true hardy perennial. I am told that the Queen of England still has her 'Valspar' raincoat, though whether it reverses to a toning floral print with a matching headscarf, I couldn't say. Everything about this useful style is classic: raglan sleeves, bust darts from the shoulder seam, neat collar and turn-back cuffs have made it the weather-proof standby of a generation.

Smartly casual

1   A fully fashioned jumper worn over ski-pants (again). It becomes smarter to wear a headscarf crossed under the chin and tied at the back of the neck, with the fringe peeping out from the pushed back scarf.

2   Another important look, that became very popular for semi-formal evening wear. A long, dark velvet skirt is worn here with a satin blouse collared with a circular-cut frill.

3   Blouse and skirt ensemble using several different toning patterns, in simple shapes that could easily be made at home.

4   This V-necked top and straight skirt was a useful alternative to the pinafore or jumper dress. It could be dressed 'up' with a frilly blouse, or 'down' with a striped pullover, as here, and worn in the office or at home depending on the fabric and the accessories.

5   The late sixties start here, not so much with the top but with the new hair-cut invented by Vidal Sassoon, and the change of emphasis in the make-up. Owl-eyes rule. The eyes were skilfully painted, using new refined make-up, to look as huge and round as possible, accented by theatrical false eyelashes. Lips became paler, to draw even more attention to the eyes.

6   Simple shirt blouse, worn with the new hipster skirt and matching frilled scarf – here tied peasant-fashion behind the head. The hipster was a difficult style for women to wear well, as it only looked smart if you didn't have any (hips, that is).

1

2

3

4

5

6

1965–70 – Vietnam versus Flower Power

The only obvious link between the American conscript to the increasingly ugly war in Vietnam and the hippy flower child was the liberal use of marijuana. Whereas the hippies took drugs to expand their minds and experience exalted levels of consciousness, to the young soldiers trapped in the flea-bitten hell-holes of the Vietnam war, drugs offered the only possible mental escape from the carnage. This unwanted war in the Far East did untold damage to America's self-image, not least because the all-conquering superpower that had rescued Great Britain in two world wars could not win its own battle.

Hippy culture and its pursuit of love, peace and psychedelia was the antithesis of 1960s main street fashion. The media gave everyone with long hair the label of 'hippy', but it was always a very loose collage of attitudes and styles. Anyone who didn't buy into the prevailing materialism, expressed by short geometric dresses and haircuts, was liable to be included in the term. Hippies admitted to roots in beatniks, folkies, surfers and psychedelics. The beats provided the link with that source of all hippiness, black jazz. The folkies gave them a vision of a simpler non-industrial communal lifestyle, and the psychedelics provided the sound and light shows, the colourful clothes and the LSD. The many sub-groups came together to express mounting horror at what was happening in Vietnam.

Youth rejected both the social and the imperialist ethos of their parents' generation, everything their elders had fought for was rejected as culturally irrelevant. For the first time in fashion history, the young led the old. The rich and grand began to ape their social inferiors. Parisian supremacy was shattered; the world looked to London for inspiration for the rest of the decade.

The enduring image of swinging London in the sixties is of young girls in mini-skirts. Inexpensive nylon tights, now widely available, allowed skirts to be far shorter than ever before without quite becoming pornographic. Reaction to this new fashion ranged from lascivious delight to moral outrage. Mary Quant has been credited with the invention of the mini-skirt. She was certainly so 'in tune' with the mood of the moment that it is her version that everyone re-members. She was one of the first designers to understand that young women no longer wanted to dress like their mothers and to design clothes specifically for the 15–25 age group, who remain an ever expanding market to this day.

Hot pants, or mini-shorts, also became popular in the mid-sixties, usually worn with tights and flat-heeled white boots. They created as much of a furore as the mini-skirt and even constituted a judicial incitement to rape.

The fashion press stated that the mini-skirt would never be seen again after its disappearance in the 1970s, but it re-emerged in a new guise, unrepentant and as sexy as ever, in the mid-eighties.

The catalysts that fired the many changes in social attitudes were the contraceptive pill and the rise of feminism. It is easy to forget the importance of these two facts. For the first time women were put in a position of control which, until now, had only been available to a privileged few. Women's new assertiveness meant that designers could no longer impose a single shape or hem length on their customers; they could only offer ideas for women to adopt or not, as they saw fit.

By 1967 the Space Age look abruptly ran out of steam. As *Vogue* put it, the pop revolution burnt out with a crackle of paper dresses. The musical *Hair* arrived in London and the Rolling Stones held a massive open-air concert in Hyde Park. These two events appeared to confirm the victory of hippy styles of dress. For most of the decade the couturiers had embraced a futuristic brutalism; it was now time for something different.

The confusion that was sixties fashion, with its futuristic looks, unisex jeans and perverse little girl clothes, gave way before the end of the decade to its complete opposite. This manifested itself as long romantic clothes from a multi-national dressing-up box. Designers stopped looking to the future for inspiration and began to plunder the world's ethnic minorities. Every culture had something to offer: Afghan coats, Mexican knitwear, American Indian beadwork, Russian peasant boots, Mandarin trousers, could be assembled with anything from India to create the look of an expensive gypsy. The fashion was ratified by the couturiers, who fought a vigorous rearguard action against the combined influences of the unstoppable growth of the ready-to-wear industry and the ever-growing stream of genuine ethnic imported garments. Sartorially speaking, the 1970s began three years early.

Couture

1   Balenciaga. Paris is still the centre of the fashion world, just. This severely elegant red tunic coat is worn with a straight skirt, wide black hat, and long black gloves. Colin McDowell considers Balenciaga to be the greatest designer of the century, who brought a Spanish sense of drama and formality to France; his mastery of cut was unsurpassed, and equalled by very few. He trained Ungaro, Givenchy and Courrèges.

2   Madame Grès originally wanted to be a sculptor, but her family considered the finer arts an unsuitable occupation for a woman so she turned to the creation of the perfectly sculptural, draped silk jersey gown. She did all her own cutting, working directly onto the mannequin with the minimum of detail and without any pattern. Always drawn to the fluid drape of jersey fabric, she worked in wool for day and silk for evening. Her clothes are so classical as to be timeless. Add carefully tousled hair and a sexy expression and this dress would not look out of place at a Hollywood awards ceremony today.

3   Sybil Connolly. Born in South Wales in 1921, Miss Connolly moved to Dublin where she started to design her own collections in 1950. Her classic lady-like clothes made her a great success in America. This finely-tucked blouse in pure Irish linen worn with a long moiré skirt became almost a uniform for country house dinners, at least in part because, most importantly for those draughty Irish castles, warm underwear could be elegantly concealed beneath.

1

2

3

Late sixties young couture

In the 1950s, all women who wore couture clothes looked at least thirty-five. In the sixties, women became girls and looked as if they had barely reached puberty. Transparent fabrics, tiny hipster skirts and boys' haircuts combed forward into heavily made-up eyes became the rage.

1　Geometric mini by Rudi Gernreich typifies this approach.

2　Courrèges, 1968. He was the most influential French designer of the sixties, with his space-age fabrics and flat, white booties. He certainly inspired a generation of futuristic costume designers but his garments were nearly unwearable in their pure form. This little dress in transparent nylon and plastic typifies the style.

3　Mini-skirt for the working girl with matching striped shoes.

4 and 5　A pair of casual outfits featuring an outsize butcher-boy cap and a huge knitted cowl collar here teamed oddly with a bare midriff. The heavy fringe, heavier clown makeup and pale lips are classic late sixties.

1

2

3

4

5

Women's day wear

1   Coat in faux Persian lamb worn by a middle-aged English woman. Countless ladies of a certain age still wear coat and skirts like this. Another example of clothes as distinct from fashion.

2   Neat short jackets were very popular. This collar detail is also very typical of the time. Here it is worn with a beret, skinny-rib polo-neck sweater and trousers in one of the new man-made crimplene fabrics.

3   The classic late-sixties coat was cut to make the wearer look as small and skinny as possible, with a childish raised waist and narrow shoulders. Here it is worn with a butcher-boy cap, neat pumps and short gloves.

4   Mandarin-collared raincoat and headscarf. Showerproof cotton poplin was made up in bright colours for weatherproof coats.

5   Another overcoat, this time cut in a slightly barrel shape with raglan sleeves, fastened with three big buttons and worn with a silk scarf tied at the back of the neck and a round furry hat.

6   Sheepskin jackets and coats were popular for both sexes. They were made with the fur side inside and obviously were very warm, much favoured for observing the grander outdoor sports such as horse racing and rugby football. The headscarf has an ingenious padded edge at the front to make a triangular piece of fabric seem a bit more formal. Also, if you were planning to go out in the evening, it hid the curlers needed for the obligatory big hairstyles.

Party clothes

1   Considering how difficult to wear late sixties clothes were for anyone over a size 8, or over the age of thirteen, it amazes me how long this image has lasted. The mid-nineties even sees a revival of little sleeveless shift dresses. This is a seminal example. The raised waist seam was designed to make the bust look as small and virginal as possible; side seams skimmed the midriff and hopefully skinny hips. The skirt ended somewhere between mid-thigh and three inches above the knee. Tights were now very popular and were nearly always the colour of tanned skin, especially for evening wear.

2   Dressy silk shantung two-piece by the Italian designer Princess Galitzine worn with a back-combed beehive hairstyle tied back and decorated with a formal matching bow on a slide; simple court shoes and, like all the models on this page, as much eye makeup as possible.

3   I think this girl is an early Jilly Cooper heroine. She wears a dark blue mini-shift dress with the flattering and ingenious bust dart invented by Barbara Hulanicki of Biba, and long open machine-lace sleeves. Her shoulder-length fair hair is back-combed. Silly earrings and tarty eye makeup contrast with the girlish figure and innocent expression.

1

2

3

Underwear and nightwear

1   Foundation garments were still reminiscent of armour plating, with pointy bras and rubber girdles still the norm. Only if you were shaped like the current model, Twiggy, could flesh be unconstrained beneath the tiny mini-dresses or crimplene ski pants. Here is a lace and stitched-nylon torpedo-shaped bra worn with a long-line pull-on in Lycra and nylon elastic net, which was supposed to flatten the tummy and upper thighs but in reality produced a curiously squashed 'mono buttock' that looked dreadful under the trousers that it was supposed to enhance.

2   Housecoat in brushed acrylic pink moufflon trimmed with pink and white yoke and cuffs. This fabric looked sweet and cuddly when new but dreadfully sad after a few washes, and has come to be associated with the unhappy image of the downtrodden cigarette-smoking wife doing the washing-up with a nylon chiffon scarf on her rollered hair, and down-at-heel fluffy slippers on her feet.

3   Mauve nylon baby-doll 'nightie-n-knicker' set worn with beribboned hair and smudged mascara. A younger and hopefully sexier version of (2).

4   Cotton bra and tiny flowered waistslip for the younger girl, sometimes worn with ...

5   ... a roll-on rubber panty girdle.

6   What nice girls wore instead of (3). Warm, unsexy (oh, the relief) flowered pyjamas in pink or blue brushed cotton winceyette.

1

2

3

4

5

6

Babies and children

1   Quilted multi-purpose suit. The idea was that the baby stayed warmly asleep in this coat-cum-sleeping-bag, but as she turned into a toddler and began to walk you unpopped the hem, and lo! the garment became a dressing gown.

2   The babygro – an all-in-one machine-washable sleep-suit that poppers down the front and through the inside leg seam for ease of access – has to be one of the most useful garments of the late twentieth century. The baby stays neat and warm whatever it does until growth and increasing mobility wear out first the knees and then the feet.

3   Winter ensemble for the small boy. A direct descendant of the fifties Harris tweed coat, with long trousers in the same fabric, are warm and comfortable. The head is covered by a curious woollen hat with a stiffened peak to stop it looking like his sister's bonnet.

4   Romper suit designed to look like a pullover and shorts in easy-care white and brown knitted Acrilan.

5   The girl's dress is a replica of an adult's (or vice versa). It has a high waist and a Peter Pan collar, and is worn with matching ribbed tights. Brightly coloured tights were more easily available for children than for adults.

6   Young boys still allowed themselves to be dressed as little men; this lad wears a drip-dry shirt, bow tie and waistcoat.

7   Zip-up anorak with fun-fur trim round the hood and hem.

1

2

3

4

5

6

7

Late sixties men

As, in the 1960s, women under forty became girls so men became boys, and they shopped in London's Carnaby Street, originally a run-down area full of the cheaper kind of tailor. Thanks to shops such as His Clothes (for Mods) and the Carnaby Cavern and I Was Lord Kitchener's Valet (for everyone else), this backwater of the grander Regent Street became, along with the King's Road, the focal point of open 'swinging London'. Clothes for the urban male quite suddenly exploded into a riot of colour and pattern, upsetting the older generation of short-haired tweed-clad men a great deal. The three examples here are a fairly representative selection.

1   Shirt with large collar in flower-print cotton with a wide matching tie worn under a hippie-style Afghan embroidered waistcoat and straight-cut hipster pants. As with the girls, big hair worn with a mop-like fringe hiding the ears was *de rigeur*.

2   Despite the fact that the *Viva Zapata* moustache was later to become a homosexual symbol, at this stage effeminacy was widely adopted by heterosexuals as a sign of sexual liberation from existing stereotypes. They could be seen in frilly satin shirts open to the waist to reveal a medallion worn on a long chain. This example goes all the way, sartorially speaking, with flared trousers made from a floral furnishing chintz and worn long enough to cover all but the toes of the zippered boots.

3   Polo-neck shirt in bright Pucci-style print.

4 and 5   Little Italian tailored suits were worn by Mods, whose style was neat, unadorned and squeaky clean. The look was typified by the matching collarless suits worn by the Beatles in their early days, who seemed so well brought-up when compared with the anarchic, sometimes cross-dressed, Rolling Stones.

Hair and accessories

Considering that the perceived memory of the sixties is of London swinging with Rock 'n' Roll, drugs and compulsory sex, I have been surprised to be reminded how sweet everybody looked. Just like Bambi really.

1   This is a nice girl going to a wedding in a *Gigi* boater hat, her shoulder-length hair waved but carefully tousled. By now hats are only worn for formal occasions such as funerals, weddings and grand social events such as Garden Parties and Royal Ascot.

2   Bobbed hair by Vidal Sassoon, false eyelashes, space-age Perspex earrings in daglo pink and orange stripes.

3   Tiny evening bag in pale leather. Short stretch gloves were available in checks or stripes.

4   Delicate sandals with the set-back medium heel typical of the period.

5   Seminal sixties look by Mary Quant. Asymmetric sharp bob by Vidal Sassoon, pale lips, enormous doe eyes, and tiny mini-dress made to look like a pinafore – in this case with a little purse stitched into its midriff, semi-opaque tights and chisel-toed shoes.

6   Owl-eyed glasses made famous by artist David Hockney.

7   Warm ribbed tights prevented the legs exposed by the mini-skirt from freezing in winter – worn here with flat-heeled white plastic boots.

8   Curious and cosy Courrèges slipper-sox. Useless as the outdoor wear for which they were designed but a good solution for trendy housewear.

9   Simple laced shoe in orange leather.

Newsreel

These drawings were taken from contemporary newsreel stills, newspapers and magazines.

1   A protester in wet weather gear: nylon kagoul jacket, jeans and wellington boots.

2   Golfer in open-necked sports shirt and flared trousers, in what used to be known as a loud check. Flat golfing shoes with large fringed tongues.

3   Off-duty singer. Longish hair, somewhere between Elvis and the Beatles, dark patterned shirt and tweed sports jacket.

4   A French film star visits America as if dressed for a society wedding, in a Chanel-style summer suit and picture hat.

5   A Canadian politician braves the hustings in a Russian sheepskin hat, wool overcoat with a beaver-fur shawl collar.

6   It was considered unpatriotic for American political wives to insist on wearing French couture instead of the home-grown version, but some were popular enough to get away with it.

CHAPTER 6

1970–75 – Retromania

The schizophrenic manifestations of fashion in the 1970s were an accurate reflection of women's uncertainty about their place in the world and of the uncertainty of the world in general. It was the decade that saw the emergence of women's lib when the chicks and dolly birds of the sixties decided that enough was enough and demanded a real piece of the social and professional action.

The movement began in 1967 in the US when Betty Friedan, in her book *The Feminine Mystique*, began to ask uncomfortable questions such as 'Who am I other than X's wife or Y's mother?' 'Man isn't the enemy,' she said to *Vogue*, 'he is the fellow victim.' – a sentiment not shared by the hard-line feminists for whom men were, indeed, the age-old enemy, agents of suppression and exploitation.

The newspapers and women's magazines enthusiastically joined in the fray. In almost every issue there was an article entitled 'The Guilt of the Working Mother' or 'How to be Super Woman'. One of the key figures was Germaine Greer, brilliant and controversial Australian writer whose book *The Female Eunuch*, published in 1970, set the stage for a decade of journalistic bickering and dinner-party debate. She argued that women did not suffer from penis-envy as Freud believed, but that centuries of patriarchal society had led to the castration and distortion of woman's natural personality. Ms Greer argued that reform was not enough, that what was needed was revolution in the social structure. Her message was profound: it was not inevitable that love led to dependence. Most men, and not a few women, found her extremely frightening, and were threatened by her explosive mix of academic rigour and full-blooded sexuality. Previously women could tentatively admit to enjoying sex, or to having a PhD – but not both.

By the seventies women over thirty had lived through more changes in fashion than at any other time in history; during the past twenty years, 'looks' had come in and, almost immediately, gone out, still apparently dictated by a small band of remote, unconcerned male designers. By the end of the sixties, women and men began to adopt a more DIY attitude to fashion; as *Vogue* expressed it, 'the real star of fashion is you – the wearer'. Women began a hunt through the fleamarkets in a search for romantic clothes from the past and from the furthest corners of the planet, and wore them all, one on top of another.

Instead of sending out signals of sexual availability, women decided to express their independence by deliberately adopting a more graceful and covered-up style of dressing. Men complained as legs were hidden by maxi-skirts, while many of us sighed with relief and vowed that our knees would never be seen in public again. As the feminist viewpoint gained momentum, women decided that the clothes of the previous decade, with their perverse air of under-age sexuality, was another way of pandering to dubious male tastes. What had begun as liberation was now seen as exploitation.

The new layered and decorated clothes were intensely romantic and expressed a great yearning for a purer, more hand-crafted past. The decorative revival spread outwards to embrace furnishings and interior decoration. In Britain the tendency begun by Biba, with its tasselled cushions and moody lamp shades, was taken up by Terence Conran of Habitat, the first and most successful of the stores that promoted a whole life style. The work of William Morris was enthusiastically revived, Sanderson reissued many of his complex and beautiful wallpaper designs, Liberty of London found itself at the cutting edge of fashion once more. Disused chapels were turned into stripped-pine warehouses where Victorian and provincial varnished or painted furniture was revitalized by immersion in a bath of caustic soda. For most of the decade it seemed that the liberal classes shopped exclusively at Habitat, Liberty and Laura Ashley.

Out-of-doors

Three coats for the seventies:

1 A natural progression from the space-age geometry of the 1960s, this winter coat was still short but proclaims its period with the novel shape of the tailored collar and the multiple buttons. The girl wears the popular, not to say ubiquitous, skinny-rib polo-neck jumper, ribbed tights and knee-length square-toed black suede boots.

2 The suburban version of the imperfectly clean embroidered goatskin worn by the better-off hippy. This cloth or suedette waisted knee-length coat is edged with wide bands of fur, usually fake. Fur-trimmed hoods were a popular addition. This girl wears slightly flared jersey trousers and square-toed boots. Her hair is a grown-out sixties bob.

3 1970s clothes could be very romantic, with long sweeping lines and softly tailored shapes. This long tweed coat was inspired by the film of *Dr Zhivago* starring Julie Christie and is worn with widely-flared trousers in shades of plum and Vandyke brown, and topped with a fur Balaclava hat.

1

2

3

Not the mini-skirt

1 Trousers became serious fashion in the 1970s. Many women preferred not to wear mini-skirts and flares; culottes or wide sailor trousers were a relaxed and, when well-cut in a sensuous fabric, glamorous alternative. Here yet another skinny-rib jumper is worn with a tailored sleeveless jerkin and modestly flared trousers, forming a usefully wearable outfit that could be dressed up or down for a number of different occasions.

2 Another two-piece, this time a V-necked, shaped tunic, worn over a silky blouse which has a typically large pointed collar and shaped sleeves, narrow round the upper arm but softly gathered round the wrists.

3 Skinny shirt in fine jersey with a small geometric pattern in two tones of the same muted colour, the darker of which is picked up in the short flared skirt.

4 Open-work fitted top, head band and ethnic jewellery.

5 Skirts became ever longer during the decade. This example is in plum-coloured needlecord and is worn with a matching Shetland wool, thigh-length cardigan, and a man's soft jersey shirt. I thought I looked very romantic and interesting in such an ensemble, as if I was going on a walking holiday in 1913 from one of the older universities!

6 Top and skirt made from three different toning printed cottons.

Accessories

1   There was a great revival of hand-crafted macramé, tie-dying, beadcraft and, above all, crochet. The ability to mix many jewel-like colours creatively became a prized skill among the alternative communities and many people had a grand-mother or auntie who could be persuaded to give up knitting pastel-toned baby blankets and concentrate on many-hued waistcoats and hats.

2   Tank top over tailored shirt blouse. Note how the corduroy flares are now brazenly zipped up the front, rather than demurely at the side.

3   Soft handbags in multi-coloured suede with shoulder straps.

4   Short gloves with a wrist strap.

5   Wigs made from nylon hair were used to cheer up your work-a-day hairstyle into something more luscious for evening. This one is styled in the fashionable layered 'lion-cut' look.

6   Strappy sandals in black patent, worn with machine lace flares.

7–9   Boots, shoes, clogs – all with solid heels and square toes.

Early seventies men

1   Men's suits did seem to look as if they were a size too small, which might be considered quite cute on the young. A pertly tailored single-breasted suit with narrow shoulders, top stitching and flares in maroon polyester mix is worn with a huge patterned tie. As in (2) and (4), the shirt has a big collar.

2   A narrow three-piece suit. Waistcoats (vests) have become fashionable again. This model is given an air of seriousness by the moustache and the over-sized spectacles, and has, like all the other sketches on this page, big hair.

3   A sports jacket in tan tweed worn over the inevitable skinny-rib polo-neck (turtle neck) sweater and flared trousers. Not all men wore flares; older men quite rightly steered clear of them for obvious reasons. They were a disaster on the short, but it was possible to buy platform-soled shoes and boots for men with 2–2½ inch heels, over which the flares were worn with just the little square toes peeping out, flatteringly giving extra height with the utmost discretion. There was, however, a small upsurge of ankle injuries among short men who had problems with the platform soles and fell off them when drunk.

4   The choirboy look, exemplified by Paul McCartney, was preferred at this time and was helped along by lots of floppy hair and the over-sized collars. Narrow shoulders accentuated the adolescent appearance and the tight patterned slip-overs made the least of the boyish chest. This mock-Fair-Isle, sleeveless, round-neck slipover was in easy-wash Acrilan.

5   Anoraks tend to have a very sad image these days, being unfairly associated with train-spotters and 'techies', but they are such useful garments, warm, waterproof and inexpensive. This example was in navy proofed cotton poplin and had a quilted lining and fur-fabric collar. A yachting cap is worn on the shoulder-length hair.

1

2

3

4

5

Vogue

1   One of the main and, in my opinion, one of the most attractive 'looks' of the seventies was this three-piece ensemble by Ossie Clark using a range of silky fabrics printed by his then partner, Celia Birtwell, here in two shades of brown on white. The use of multiple patterns in one outfit was very popular and, if used with a sure eye, original and interesting. Although ever more popular during the day, the wearing of trousers for evening still caused comment as, indeed, in some circles it still does.

2   Also by Ossie Clark, American Indian cut and fringed soft caramel suede jacket and skirt. Perfectly in tune with the growing Political Correctness of interest in indigenous cultures, this suit makes a change from the many Asian garments that were beginning to be seen in the European market.

3   Romantic long top and skirt in richly patterned fabrics by the great textile designer, Bernard Neville, who was the head of design at Liberty. Designers such as Belleville Sassoon and Thea Porter encouraged the love of dressing up in dresses of 'antique splendour' decorated with lace and gold cord. These gently feminine clothes also made splendidly exotic maternity garments.

1

2

3

Laura Ashley and Jean Muir

1   Laura Ashley was the first of the so-called 'life-style' designers. Her clothes were the antithesis of the sharp, modern and angular sixties. They were made of washable one-hundred-per-cent cotton in small all-over prints in soft colours and usually had long, gathered skirts and demure necklines finished with a lace collar. The effect was of an English Edwardian summer, with angelic children gathering strawberries in sailor-collared dresses and pinafores while their mothers dispensed home-made lemonade in sun-hats and consciously 'old-fashioned' dresses.

Laura Ashley's dresses were never high fashion but they had enormous appeal for the liberal middle classes, embodying, as they did, a more innocent, less relentlessly sexy age.

2   Home-spun walking outfit in cream knit, including a hand-knitted Aran sweater tied round the middle, Fair Isle cap, mittens and socks, worn with warm walking boots. Apart from the boots, this ensemble might have been warm but was hardly practical, as it made no attempt to be shower-proof and the cream pants would have become entangled on the first gorse bush.

3   Jean Muir's detractors complained that she designed the same dress for thirty years. Certainly her signature style remained unusually consistent. She usually worked in a wonderful fabric called Hure Jersey in moody bruise colours and her clothes involved intricate body-skimming cutting, reminiscent of the great dressmakers of the 1930s. Miss Muir insisted on technical expertise of a very high order and was regularly on record as complaining that there was too much art and not nearly enough craft among her younger (British) competitors. She was right, of course, but her disciplined perfectionism was always too austere for the more ephemeral tastes of the speedy young. She is remembered as one of England's greatest fashion designers and, a small but significant point, I have never, ever, found one of her dresses or beautiful suede coats in a charity shop — their owners keep them for life.

1

2

3

Tory lady and guru

1 In 1970 the Beatles went to India to seek enlightenment at the feet of the Maharishi, leader of the Spiritualist Regeneration Movement, after being introduced to him by George Harrison's wife, Patti. Along with many other westerners, disenchanted by materialism and the stranglehold of scientific rationalism, they were taught the secrets of transcendental meditation and the Oneness of All. George Harrison learned to play the sitar.

The Maharishi himself wore the traditional flowing garments of the Indian *guru* or holy man; his followers designed garments for themselves using India-made shirts and caftans which had become increasingly available in the west.

2 and 3 I remember many of the Beatles fans feeling rather betrayed when the embarrassingly named Fab Four outgrew their little matching suits and began to appear in ethnic garments garnished with flowers, worry beads and beards. Clean-cut and well-behaved compared with the pop stars that followed them, their need for spiritual growth was seen as a slap in the face of the culture that had produced them and proved conclusively that the sixties were definitely over.

4 It is hard to believe that this style is from the same year. This is a Conservative woman MP in summer. She wears rigidly set bouffant hair, a touch of lipstick and powder, two rows of pearls, a straight sleeveless dress in a nice, bright print with a pussy-cat bow, a very hard handbag (for self defence?), tan tights and neat court shoes. She embodies everything that the Beatles were rejecting, and some seventeen years of the triumph of her and her kind is at hand.

Maternity

1   This excellent dress was advertised as being 'suitable before, during and after pregnancy'. Few women were willing to invest in a complete new wardrobe now that they were not condemned to bear dozens of babies, so maternity clothes needed to be practical as well as attractive.

2   The pretty, child-like smocks, here in white cotton and Indian lace, were perfect for pregnancy, even if they did make the mother-to-be look too young to be bearing children. Flared trousers came supplied with an elastic tummy panel to accommodate the bulge.

3   Andy-Pandy or clown's dungarees were an innovation that is still worn by the younger mum-to-be. The bulge is now beginning to be celebrated rather than hidden away. Here it is combined with a pretty long-sleeved blouse in a floral print lawn and a simple straw sun-hat.

1

3

2

CHAPTER 7

1975–80 – Rise of the New Woman

In February 1975 Margaret Thatcher became the first woman to lead the Conservative Party and in May 1979 she became Britain's first female Prime Minister. She ruled the country, the Tory Party and her ministers with an obsessive single-minded determination for twelve and a half years, doing as little as possible for the rights of other women. Intellectually and socially Mrs Thatcher was the exact opposite of the writer and lecturer Germaine Greer. Between them, they succeeded in polarizing Britain into two camps, each with its own distinct style of dress. In the late seventies Ms Greer's faction was dominant. The standard response from the defensive male was to assume that Ms Greer and her sisters were man-hating lesbians. In many revolutionary movements it is necessary for the pendulum to swing as far as it will go in the new direction and a significant number of women did class men as the supreme enemy; burnt their bras, ceased to shave their legs and went to bed with each other. No attitude went unquestioned, each item of apparel was considered for its political correctness. Any item that could be perceived as man-pleasing or designed to keep woman in her place was discarded to be replaced by sexless dungarees and flat shoes. These committed, but unfortunately somewhat humourless, women were easy objects of ridicule even by other women.

For the many Englishwomen who declined to get involved with all these upheavals, the favourite shop was Laura Ashley. Mrs Ashley was one of the greatest of the so-called life style designers; almost by default, for in her case the life style came first and the clothes second. She began her fashion career designing simple printed cottons on her Welsh farmhouse table, going on to have her demure feminine clothes made up by local women and selling them from a single shop in the Fulham Road. As a committed Christian she felt that too much liberation led inevitably to sinful promiscuity, so she offered women and children a charming alternative aesthetic which evoked a sunlit pastoral idyll of an endless family country picnic. Coming as it did at a time of profound social unease, her ideas were immensely seductive and, thanks to the sound business sense of her husband Major Bernard Ashley, the firm prospered and the shops multiplied.

Long dresses for semi-formal and formal evening occasion were very popular in the late seventies. Every kind of ethnic influence was utilized and every magazine advertised its caftan, muumuu or kimono as the latest solution for comfortable and glamorous dinner wear. Designers plundered books normally only used by theatre costumiers for new shapes inspired by Moroccan wedding garments or Ukrainian peasants. Cleaned up, sometimes made in synthetic fabrics and generally westernized, these garments were translated everywhere, from the highest couture to the most commonplace mail-order catalogue.

Perhaps nothing expresses the great diversity of the decade more clearly than a list of the popular shows and films. They divided into escapism through nostalgia (*Death in Venice*, *The Boyfriend*), violence (*Rollerball*, *Carrie* and *The Exorcist*), nostalgia and violence (*Bonnie and Clyde*, *The Godfather*). Dance films such as *Cabaret* and *Saturday Night Fever* and shows such as *A Chorus Line* sent people rushing to the dance studios to learn how to do it themselves. The increasing fascination with other worlds was best expressed by Steven Spielberg's *Close Encounters of the Third Kind*.

As inflation grew and the dole queues lengthened, the cinema's hopeful message of spiritual renewal struck a deep chord in an increasingly materialistic world.

Bill Gibb and Biba

1   In 1977 Bill Gibb was awarded the astonishing accolade of a retrospective exhibition at the Royal Albert Hall at the very young age of thirty-four. A year later he had to cease trading. New backers were found but Gibb was bankrupted again a few years later, and by 1988 he was dead of what, among creative people, has become chillingly known as 'the usual' – Aids.

This brilliant and much-loved designer was known for his gloriously coloured and intricately patterned knitwear and his extravagant evening and bridal wear. His occasion dresses were genuinely beautiful and original – made to a standard not seen since the Edwardian era from where much of his inspiration came. They were naturally extremely expensive, but must have been so costly to produce that Gibb's profit margins were too low for commercial survival. His knitwear was designed in collaboration with the superb colourist Kaffe Fasset. This ensemble was available in autumn shades or in denim blues and greys. Very desirable indeed.

2   Kimono, top and harem pants in fine cream jersey. The use of well-mixed ethnic influences was a trademark of the seventies. The kimono is decorated with more geometric patterned braid.

3   Silky suit from Biba, in one of Celia Birtwell's exquisite border prints. The slimming cut, with narrow shoulders and thighs and long flared sleeves and trousers, made girls look like very young rag dolls.

1

2

3

Women's clothes

1   This easy-shaped dress has semicircular sleeves and a long skirt gathered onto a raised lace-covered waistband. The style remained popular as night-wear.

2   The best-selling summer dress from Marks & Spencer in 1977. It was made in white, caramel and coffee-coloured crinkle cotton cheesecloth, which, along with velvet, was the hippies' favourite fabric. The drawstring top is shaped like a peasant blouse and the mid-calf length skirt is gathered in bands of increasing fullness, all cut perfectly straight. This girl wears a simple straw sun-hat and wedge-heel espadrilles, and carries her belongings in a coloured straw bag, hand-embroidered with raffia flowers.

3   High-waisted dress with grown on short sleeves and open collar. It has an insertion of printed 'folk' embroidery.

4   Long, rather medieval dress for dining at home. Made in flowing crêpe, it is finished with machine-embroidered neckline, sleeves and waistband.

5   Gypsy garments that would have been very surprising to most gypsies. The headscarf is tied peasant-fashion at the nape of the neck over curly hair. The dress is of several different prints, often in soft cotton or viscose and trimmed with cord, ric-rac braid and coloured ribbon.

6   This floaty evening dress was a joy for the larger woman; indeed such garments are so comfortable and attractive that in various fabrics they are still a mainstay of the well-endowed or those who have a middle rather than a waist.

1

2

3

4

5

6

Accessories

1 Matching woolly hat, scarf and gloves in a colourful geometric-patterned knit. These were made rather expensively in beautifully coordinated Shetland wools or, more affordably, in man-made fibres.

2 There was a vogue for sensible brogue lace-up shoes, to go with all that home-spun tweed and hand-made knits. This example is rendered very un-sensible by the addition of a four-inch (10 cm) heel.

3 Almost every shoe style received the high-wedge-sole treatment. Here a brown suede running shoe is given a three-inch (8 cm) heel in composition crêpe.

4 Hostess apron in checked cotton, edged and trimmed with contrasting colour. I think they were called 'hostess' because they were pretty enough to be revealed to guests, as distinct from the messy old thing in which you actually did the cooking.

5 Even bikini swimsuits could now be made in denim-look with the addition of a little Lycra. Simple bra top and brief shorts in faded blue with top-stitching.

6 Kimono style house-coat in red and white sprigged polycotton, trimmed with red.

7 The world was amazed when, in the early nineties, Vivienne Westwood produced towering platform shoes – but they were not new. Here are the outrageous originals.

A rather arty wedding

1   The bride, who didn't want to wear 'fancy dress', wears an ivory crêpe silk blouse and tussah silk, gored skirt. The narrow-shouldered jacket was made from a Victorian cream silk shawl, with pale flowers and a long fringe.

2   The groom, a musician (which explains everything), defies convention by wearing a brown floral silk shirt, suede jacket and pale pin-stripe flared trousers. It may be of interest that this bridegroom appears in a very conventional Harris tweed coat, aged three, on page 15.

3   As does his mother. Here she wears a matching coral pink jacket and sleeve-less dress. Her hat is covered with white daisies and she wears a pearl necklace and light brown court shoes.

4   The father of the bride is in an elderly black morning coat and pleat-front pin-stripe trousers, brought up to date by a brocade waistcoat and spotted tie.

5   Wedding guest. He wears a fashionable brown velvet suit with narrow, rather pointed shoulders and flared trousers, a cornflower blue silk shirt and floppy bow tie.

1

2

3

4

5

Pop singer and groupie

1   Hippie-influenced summer wear. This girl wears a drawstring cheesecloth top, with bare midriff. Her long straight hair is tied with a long, fringed scarf in the same soft striped fabric as the full, gathered trousers. Her shoes are wedge-heeled sandals.

2   An observing artist wears owl-eye spectacles, blue shirt and gaily striped tie.

3   A fan of the Osmonds, the Mormon family who became that unusual phenomenon, a successful Christian pop group. Donny, the oldest and the prettiest, inspired special devotion in pre-pubescent girls. This fan wears a home-crocheted bonnet-like hat, a suede shirt-jacket covered with badges and rosettes of the Beloved, a T-shirt printed with faces of the same, and, of course flared denim jeans, with soft drawstring bag and laced platform shoes.

4   Androgyny rules. This pop star deliberately creates gender confusion by choosing traditionally feminine silks and satins in bright jewel colours and using a narrow-shouldered blouse with puffed sleeves to create a slim, unmanly torso and tight-to-the-knee hipster flares to show off the boyish buttocks. High-heeled square-toed zipped boots in patchworked leather complete the much-imitated look.

1

2

3

4

Montana

1 and 2   The eighties begin in 1979 with these designs by Claude Montana: a cheerful sailor suit for real life and an outrageous outfit inspired by futuristic Japanese armour for the unreal variety. One wonders how many of these black leather helmets actually sold; I could certainly use them in my next production of *Atilla* but, for a business lunch in the neighbourhood bistro, I think not.

These two ensembles are perfect examples of 'cuspoid' design in that they point the way that mainstream fashion will go. Buyers and fashion editors use their intuitive skill to pick the directional pieces out of the multitude of ideas thrown up by the couturiers. Very few women want to dress like a Japanese warrior but the shape is important. Both outfits have massive shoulders, achieved by shoulder pads unused since the 1940s, natural waistlines and narrow-hipped pants – in other words an exact inversion of the 1970s silhouette.

3   This is what real women are still wearing in the evening. Green chiffon cut in circles is used over a slender shift for this softly pretty layered dress. The soppy seventies are about to be superseded by the aggressive eighties.

1

2

3

Tailoring

1 and 2   The fashions of any decade seem to start a year or two ahead of the end of the previous ten years. The glossy magazines got bored with flopsy ethnic layering, and quite suddenly men started to look like conventionally tailored men again – and, from the evidence of these pictures sketched from a 1976 *Vogue*, so did the girls.

Inspired by actresses Katherine Hepburn and Greta Garbo, designers began producing soft cashmere coats and man-tailored pants suits, which really were rather a relief after the endless floral and velvet bits and pieces of the earlier 1970s.

3   This Scottish artist wears a corduroy jacket and single-breasted collared waistcoat, much as artistic men did in the 1950s. The date is proclaimed by the longish hair and the tie-less shirt.

4   The Italian male never really became enthusiastic about embroidered waistcoats or velvet flares, always preferring the more virile look of a well-tailored suit. And, once men decided that exploiting the traditional right-wing capitalism was the smart way to live, so fashion dressed them for the part in double-breasted suits and gangster-ish overcoats.

1

2

3

4

Frills and fins

1   Janice Wainright designs a finale to seventies dressing, while prefiguring the Japanese influence of the early eighties. She called this a 'pagoda' dress, reflecting the way the stitching stiffens the hems of the antique-pleated silk and causes them to flip out as the layers spiral from yoke to ground. The square-cut yoke seems to be formed from pieces of Chinese embroidery – table mats, perhaps? The style begins to redefine the way women look, as it takes no notice of the conventional sexy bits but is not in the least aggressive.

2   The rise of Giorgio Armani from a brilliant man's tailor to the most copied designer of the 1980s starts here. The suit is built and structured with military precision, a point of departure that would evolve and deconstruct during the next fifteen years.

3   Mermaid dress with finny sleeves by Thierry Mugler. Mugler's instinct that any woman with a figure wanted to look like a transvestite about to receive an Oscar proved to be triumphantly correct. Women of the eighties didn't want to look like 'ladies' any more and this showy, slippery sequinned sheath points the way. The hair, borrowed from Mrs Frankenstein, is interesting.

1

3

2

CHAPTER 8

1980–85 – Swing to the Right

In 1980 the ex-actor Ronald Reagan became President of the United States. He and his wife Nancy spearheaded a lurch to the right, mirroring the activities of Margaret Thatcher in Britain. His policies contributed to the destruction of the social welfare system, greatly increased the gap between rich and poor. When it is fashionable to be rich, middle-aged and right-wing, the more adventurous style of the artistic liberal is not appreciated. Clothes became couture-led, traditionally glamorous and ostentatiously expensive. Shabby chic has no place in smart Republican society!

The technological advances that accelerated during the 1980s, combined with political trends, brought great changes. To the horror of gently liberal parents, ambitious twenty-somethings took over the City and Wall Street, advertising and the banks, with one aim – to make large sums of money. Property became ever more expensive, with house prices in fashionable areas doubling every five years. Yuppies (Young Urban Professionals) took out enormous mortgages at usurious interest rates, and then paid for improvements and redecorating by credit card which also charged high interest rates. It helped to be a DINKY (Dual Income No Kids Yet) to pay for this lifestyle.

Urban life moved into fast forward mode, abetted by the computer, the telephone answering machine and the fax. Commodity brokers and share dealers rose early to catch news of the Tokyo stock market, metropolitan restaurants were full of executives starting their day with multiple power breakfasts, women took on management positions and jogged or worked out before going to the office, having made an appointment to dine with their husband in a smart multi-national restaurant. Yuppies dined out several times a week since Mrs Yuppie had little time to cook. High-class convenience food, freshly prepared and ready to pop into the microwave oven, was expensive but time-saving. When our yuppie couple had any energy left over for procreation, their smart, well-oiled life suffered some tremendous shocks.

Without a job the new mother could not afford to look after her child; the mortgage repayments were too high for one income and anyway, it was difficult enough for a woman to retain her place in the pecking order, and to re-enter the job market after a child-rearing gap meant a drastic drop in status

10. A child's dress by Clothkits (*left*),
an Indian print maternity dress, and a child's
dress by Laura Ashley 1976

11. Unwithered by age – in pink, 1977

14. New looks from Japan
by Issy Miyake 1983

15. Summer evening dress
by Bill Blass 1984

16. Three little black dresses 1990

and earnings – so many women forced their softened bodies back into their black power suits and returned guiltily to work, relying on substitute child carers to look after their offspring.

It is true that the indigenous domestic servant class is a thing of the past, but the growing number of affluent family units, where the adults are out all day, provoked a whole range of freelance operators who offered a bewildering range of household services to be paid for by the hour. A quick glance at the classified advertisements of a woman's magazine gives some idea of the crafts and trades available. Alongside advertisements for cooks, party chefs and cleaners, were artisans of every kind who would stencil, sponge and rag roll walls or furniture, muralists to create fantasy landscapes in your dining room, makers of curtains, including swags and roman blinds, upholsterers, gardeners, persons who would walk your dog, water the house plants, do your shopping, buy the Christmas presents, sort out your wardrobe; the list is endless, but the shift in work practices is clear. As full time work became more and more difficult to obtain, many people took up these services as the only available option. In other words, either the woman or her partner employed a range of part-time professionals to organize their life or she stayed home and did the lot herself like a good 1950s wife.

The 1980s saw the spectre of Aids spread across the West. The virus is thought to have originated, like humanity itself, in Central Africa, from where it may have spread by 'sexual tourists' bringing it back with them to the West. The bath houses of San Francisco were the centre of an exuberant and flourishing gay culture, where transvestite roller skating nuns consorted with Californian beach boys in cut-off jeans, media men who all looked like Burt Reynolds, boys from all the creative professions and apparently straight family men enjoying an evening off. By the end of the decade Aids was one of the biggest killers of young men in America, and the small red ribbon worn on the lapel at all media functions became a universally acknowledged reminder of this grim fact.

American fashion

1   Paris and Milan had *haute couture* and London led the way in street couture but it was the Americans who actually got it right. Following Claire McCardell and Bonnie Cashin in the forties and fifties, these brilliant and perceptive designers have produced relaxed and beautiful clothes that exactly fit the life style of their customers. Their simplicity is such that copies and 'rip-offs' can be on the rails a fortnight after the trade shows. Not that this Halston evening ensemble could be copied in a hurry. The sumptuous sequinned chiffon involved weeks of work by some underpaid immigrant, but the pared-down super-simple shape is a true classic and could, indeed can, be worn successfully by any woman regardless of her age and shape. Halston's speciality was slinky and very sexy Hollywood gowns, much worn to Oscar award ceremonies.

2   Oscar de la Renta, a giant of the East Coast social scene, is perhaps the most European of the great American designers, his name resting on his richly opulent women's clothes. This 1983 black silk organza tiered dress with an embroidered faille bolero is inspired by flamenco dancers.

3   Perry Ellis, Geoffrey Beene, Calvin Klein and Ralph Lauren have become mainstays of the home-dressmaker pattern books, as their good, simple shapes are easy to make well but surprisingly difficult to reproduce cheaply.

    Ellis has the clean-cut college boy look so admired by his countrymen and women and regarded with some suspicion by Europeans. His clothes are amazingly influential. This cropped red jacket and Oxford pants, hat, scarf and spats in four different patterns is witty and very wearable.

4   A simple cocktail dress by John Anthony in 1981. Like Klein and Lauren, he is a minimalist who produces a sleek look for the top end of the ready-to-wear market.

5   Perry Ellis again; the directional suit of the eighties. Versions of this easy three-piece must be in every woman's wardrobe, either as a suit or as separates. This version has no details at all, except unseen shoulder pads. The almost-ankle-length skirt, in this case knife-pleated, is the kindest hemline of all and, whatever Paris or London may say, sells more than any other; and the long unstructured jacket, though lovely on the skinny, is a gift to the better-endowed.

6   Another perfect classic look, by Klein, so straightforward that it can hardly be said to be designed at all. Although conceived for long-limbed American girls,

this shirt jacket and long pleated skirt in linen chambray has become the main-stay of every chainstore from California to Berlin — what you wear when you don't feel like wearing fashion!

The British version

1   English designers bring a much-needed dash of humour into a vast and often turgid business. Unfortunately the witty and unstructured often slips into scruffiness and mess. Stevie Stewart, barely out of the Middlesex Polytechnic, was running her design house, Body Map, at the age of twenty-five. She and her partner, David Holah, epitomized the eighties climate of Thatcherite opportunity that provided government loans to the very young to start innovative businesses. Unfortunately the fashion mainstream was hardly welcoming to the newcomers, although perfectly happy to exploit their bright and comfortable ideas.

2   Wendy Dagworthy designed this oversized T-shirt and has remained a long-lasting success, owing to her finely tuned instinct for what young women actually wear. Note the use of hockey boots in black canvas, an unheard-of idea but inevitable given the universal adoption of sports training shoes for casual wear.

3   This easy layered outfit by Betty Jackson is so laid back as to be virtually anti-fashion. Although the look didn't last on the catwalks, I have drawn it large because in various forms the granddad shirt, unstructured jacket and pleated mid-calf skirt are now as much a part of late-twentieth-century dress as blue jeans.

The Japanese view

This is the way twentieth-century fashion could have gone but didn't. I well remember the consternation when the brilliant Japanese designers burst upon the couture scene. Their clothes were like nothing ever seen before, a complete re-working of western fashion seen through eyes brought up on origami and 3,000 years of the kimono. Journalists loved them for their originality but the influential buyers were nervous and called it 'bag-lady' fashion; with some reason, it must be said, for any mistake with the difficult asymmetric cut and over-sized proportions and conventional notions of well-bred tidiness went out of the window.

1   Matsuda. Western outfit designed on Japanese principles. The use of shapeless over-garments and rumpled leggings was not generally appealing.

2–5   Outfits by the eminently influential Yohji Yamamoto, born 1943. Trained in Japan in all aspects of the clothing industry and, like Kawakuto of Comme des Garçons, he is in the forefront of that 'new' dressing which refuses to titillate by exposing the female form in a conventional way. His clothes confuse fifteen years later just as much as they did at the time but the concept of the unstructured garment had a huge influence on all those who disliked the eighties power suit, with its padded shoulders and revealing Lycra 'body' – the look that did define the mainstream (see page 169).

Eighties couture

1   If the Japanese designers were shocking eccentrics, the nervy Yves St Laurent is the designer who perhaps most exactly defines the main thrust of fashion. This ensemble became the most copied shape of the decade. The neat boxy jacket with its padded shoulders and straight knee-length skirt was the mainstay of every working woman's wardrobe for years. It exactly filled the new, hard-edged right-wing concept of Reagan's America and Thatcher's Britain. Rigid and uncomfortable as these suits were, they became a uniform, in much the same way as a man's business suit.

2   Sonia Rykiel creates an equally influential alternative look in soft cashmere jersey. This two-piece is in powder blue, a colour not much used in *haute couture*; it is difficult to make it look dramatic but it is very much worn in 'real life'. Shoulder pads become the trade mark of the decade; if you were not careful you could end up wearing three pairs, little ones in a blouse, larger in the jacket of your business suit and absolutely enormous in your greatcoat, making perfectly normal women look like top-heavy American footballers.

3   Jean-Louis Cherre created this rather theatrically furred and embroidered beige cashmere coat. This Russian look was also much copied, in cheaper fabrics and fake fur.

1

2

3

Englishmen and yuppies

Clothes for men in the 1980s expressed the right-wing political climate with great accuracy. The left-over hippies and rock-star wannabes either went underground and adopted New Age spiritual values or cut their hair, bought a suit, went to the gym and joined in with the real business of the eighties – making large sums of money. The gap between the haves and have-nots became wider than ever and the Young Urban Professional or yuppie was born.

1 The bomber jacket re-emerged as an all-purpose jacket, this time with fur fabric collar and footballer's shoulder pads. Shirt collars shrank, seemingly overnight, and all those patterned flares were banished to the ever-increasing number of charity shops, to become objects of great hilarity among the young and – a decade later – desirable collectors' items.

2 Towelling robe, after bath, after shower and after sport, replaced the traditional dressing gown for all but the most determinedly old-fashioned.

3 Short-sleeved plaid shirt worn over a white T-shirt with 'chino' trousers which became the only acceptable summer alternative to jeans. Chinos were basic American army fatigues and brought a welcome change from all that blue denim.

4 The trainer – the shoe of the eighties, worn by men, women and children for all but formal occasions. Children bullied their parents until the desired brand was purchased or acceptable 'rip-offs' were acquired at the local market; the most popular brands were very expensive, and the tyranny of the trainer lasted until kids decided they were ready for Doc Marten boots. Trainers, though still ludicrously over-designed and over-priced, have now stopped being an all-purpose fashion garment and have reverted to the sportsfield and the gym.

5 Two-piece suit in lightweight wool tweed. Shoulders have small pads that increased in size throughout the decade, until finally they collapsed altogether. Here the narrow lapels and single button are reminiscent of late 1950s tailoring. Many men never wore suits at all now, but the yuppie in the City or in international banking needed to dress the part, in a good, sober navy or charcoal suit.

6 The rural and suburban version. Great Britain was overrun with olive green waxed cotton made by the old country clothing company of Barbour. The British landed gentry, all farmers, chaps who hunted, shot or merely drank in the outer suburbs – all wore Barbour jackets – clean, with shoes, if you were just visiting, or absolutely filthy with wellies if you were the 'real thing'.

1

2

3

4

5

6

Children

1   This girl wears an all-purpose, unisex, leisure suit of polycotton brushed jersey. In heavier weights such suits were worn for sports and play and the less robust, more brightly coloured versions were for night wear.

2   Small boy's suit. Top in bright blue with red sleeves with some boyish logo on the chest and matching pants. His baseball cap advertises some favourite team or the latest pre-teen movie and on his feet are small expensive trainers.

3   Practical toddlers' clothes were washable, cheerful and non-iron. When Mother has no household help, endless small garments that need hand-laundering or ironing are simply unacceptable for all but the most special occasions. This little boy wears a polo-collared top, bib-and-brace dungarees and trainers – this time fastened with Velcro.

4   The craze during the early eighties was roller-skating and the mostly American-made skates had large plastic wheels bolted onto the rigid sole of the specially designed boot. Along with skate-boarding – and later roller-blading – this rather dangerous pastime spawned specialist shops that supplied knee and elbow pads, gloves and lightweight helmets against the inevitable tumbles.

5   In 1984 it was the justifiably proud boast of our local state primary school that every pupil had been taught to swim by their eleventh birthday. As education became less adequately funded, especially in hard-pressed inner city areas, compulsory swimming was one of the first activities to be lost. Swimming is still an enormously popular pastime, however, and sensible, stretchy one-piece suits are the most acceptable wear.

6   Simple cotton jersey summer dress in blue and white. The vest-shaped top and gathered short skirt could hardly be less fussy, worn here with Lolita-style heart-shaped plastic sunglasses, canvas sandals and hair tied up with bright stretchy bands.

Underwear and shoes

1 and 2   Underwired bras. Both have a plunge neckline to show off the cleavage and the one on the left has moulded cups edged with lace. Shoulder pads could be purchased separately should your new top be made without them; they were made from foam rubber and could be tucked under the bra straps.

3   Oversized T-shirts are the most comfortable garments to sleep in and many are sold especially for the purpose, often decorated with cartoon characters.

4   Bra-and-pants set in nylon and Lycra. The bra cups are pre-formed to give a smooth natural line under lightweight tops. Briefs became available in ever briefer shapes until, for the bold, they were little more than strippers' thongs – perhaps to counteract the unisex clothes that went on top.

5   Shoes followed two distinct styles. High heels enjoyed a renaissance, in classic court or T-strap shapes. On the other hand, for casual wear comfortable shoes for women became smart as well as politically correct.

6   Wedge-heel sandal, worn in warm weather and sometimes as a house-shoe for those who are allergic to bedroom slippers.

7   Sandal based on a Roman or gladiator shoe. These look interesting with long skirts in Indian fabrics as an alternative to the seventies espadrille.

8   Serious walking shoes evolved with the comfort of trainers but in unpolished leather, often using two or three colours, for those who felt that sports shoes should only be used for sport. Shoes such as these have become immensely popular for country wear and, in more sophisticated colours, or black, for women of a certain age for everyday non-office wear.

Business suits

The eighties was the decade when it was 'cool' to be right-wing. Ronald Reagan at least pretended to support the arts (as an ex-actor he could hardly do otherwise).

1   Women who held positions of power wore, and still wear, suits such as this. Apart from the strange Elizabethan shoulders with their pleated 'head' and stiffened epaulettes, the cut is simple neo-Chanel with its bound edges and not-too-tight straight skirt. The blouse with its floppy silk bow added a feminine touch, businesslike but not too threatening. Mrs Thatcher adopted versions of this style and it instantly became very threatening indeed.

2 and 3   Power-dressing for the New Woman or female yuppie. These uncompromising suits were worn by women who insisted on being taken seriously in the still overwhelmingly masculine worlds of business and the law. The idea was to play the game according to the old rules, so as not to give men any excuse to indulge in sexist or patronizing behaviour that any overtly feminine display of thigh or cleavage might induce. Therefore, for the office, hair is beautifully cut or, if long, tied back in a braid or chignon. The suit is rigidly tailored with square masculine shoulders in traditional 'business' colours of navy, charcoal grey and ever more black. A shirt or blouse is worn, often in white or cream. Skirts are straight and of varying length but getting shorter as the decade progresses. Most women under fifty wore opaque black tights and flat black shoes for work. Straight pants became an acceptable alternative to the skirt but some professions insisted that women should not wear them.

1

2

3

CHAPTER 9

1985–90 – Power dressing and the New Man

If I have devoted an entire chapter to the Aggressive Yuppie culture, it is because their frenetic energy, until the stock market crash of 1987, made them disproportionately visible. In fact, black-clad designer executives were simply a noisy group which did indeed define the mainstream, but which was only one of a multitude of different style tribes, each with its own uniform and function. These tribes overlapped, shifted and interlocked, for many individuals belonged to more than one group, changing their image to suit the activity of the moment.

A major influence on late twentieth-century fashion and anti-fashion has been Vivienne Westwood and her long-standing partner, Malcolm McLaren. Throughout the seventies, Westwood and McLaren took their inspiration from anarchic urban youth and turned it first into street style and, subsequently, into high fashion. To begin with, their clothes were based around leather and rubber fetishism, bondage and S & M. They invented punk dressing, which was disseminated by McLaren through his pop groups, especially the Sex Pistols. McLaren made the startling claim that music is an extension of fashion and should be sold as such. It is certainly true that each stylistic group has a symbiotic relationship with its preferred music; the former may easily be deduced from the latter, and vice versa.

It is interesting to note that the nihilistic punks and the pushy yuppies were both in reaction from their parents' generation many of whom were our old friends the hippies. As the mainstream became ever more obsessed with power, personal wealth and selfish materialism, so the Age of Aquarius, prefigured in the sixties, now flowered in earnest with a rapidly growing interest in the things of the spirit. The many aspects of this movement can be found conveniently gathered under the roof of The Festival of Mind, Body and Spirit. There you will find stalls offering books on channelling, yoga and creative visualization; others selling crystals of every kind with instructions as to their special properties; homeopathic and herbal medicines, dispensed with the aid of a handheld pendulum; handmade meditation stools and CDs of Tibetan overtone chanting. Other cubicles contain practitioners of every kind of Eastern massage system, spiritual healers, or Kirlian photographers. Visiting speakers claim to be able to regress a room full of people back to an awareness of their past lives, and musicians practise ecstatic singing while accompanying themselves on assorted ethnic instruments. The whole experience, ranging from profoundly life-changing to the downright silly, is, in its various forms, an expression of what has come to be called the New Age.

Right at the other end of the spiritual spectrum are the fundamentalists, such as born-again Christians and hard-line Moslems. Although it is easy to be dismissive of simplistic belief systems, religious fundamentalism is a fastgrowing force to be reckoned with. At its best it promotes secure old fashioned values and a strong sense of community at a time when the divorce rate is soaring and the family is under threat.

Eighties street style

Two Goths and a Punk

1 and 2   Goths, like Dracula, have had remarkable staying power as a style tribe. While most young people look for amusement, there will always be a few who are more at ease with the stylish and romantic vision of a life in the shadow of death. The inspirations of Dracula, Vampires and the Munsters have produced some remarkable images, driven by a strong mystical philosophy. The colour for clothes is black, black and more black; the fabrics are velvet, lace and leather, with corsets, silver jewelry and spiky heeled shoes or boots. Make-up for both sexes consists of white pancake skin, with theatrical black and purple eyes and lips. The black dyed hair is teased upwards as far as it will go (hers) or gelled flat with a shaved or painted window's peak (his). This cult has great staying power. Polhemus conjures the sweet image of a couple of Goths huddled protectively together in almost every village in England. Indeed, the pair we know used to huddle a great deal and were wont to spend summer nights encouraging their children to listen to the vibes of pre-historic burial chambers.

3   The word 'punk' was used by Shakespeare and is one of the many synonyms for prostitute. In North American slang it means inferior or worthless. If Vivienne Westwood and Malcolm McLaren did not invent the word, they are certainly credited with the invention of the style. Ted Polhemus feels that its true origins are American, and that it only reached Britain once its alien qualities were established. The punk's belief system is essentially nihilistic, with the despairing cry of 'No future!' as its rallying call. Punks countered the love and dyed-hippie culture, which itself was a revolt against the previous generation. They were an all-too evocative expression of the economic stagnation and rising unemployment of Margaret Thatcher's Britain.

Visually the torn rag-bags of black leather, grubby T-shirts and faded denim with DMs and chains take second place to the extraordinary treatment of the hair. The scalp was often shaved except for a 'Mohican'-style ridge running from brow to nape. This ridge would be bleached, dyed a bright rainbow colour, then gelled into a rigid fan that both startled and shocked the casual observer. Indeed, many punks relied on their fantastic appearance to beg from bewildered tourists.

1

2

3

Summer casuals

1   For ten years it was impossible to buy a woman's top without shoulder pads. The overall silhouette was that of the American Football player, an inverted triangle, which, when combined with this casual summer style that appears to be based on that of an off-duty GI, was cross-dressing in all but name. The over-size jacket, embellished with storm flaps, pockets and assorted straps in khaki cotton, is worn with matching pants cut with a jeans-like basque but with pleats springing from the hip seam. The T-shirt has a logo on it; along with shoulder pads, it became quite difficult to buy leisure garments without some form of advertising slogan or emblem printed across the chest.

2   A vest or tank-top with cut away back, only wearable by those with no breasts or who had 'worked out' so much that they had no need of a bra. Spiky urchin hair cut and chinos.

3   Oversized shirt of military cut, cinched into the waist with a wide elastic belt, matching straight mid-calf skirt with a slit up the back. Long tumbling fair-streaked hair.

4   Cotton summer dress with a wrap-over back and longish skirt of unpressed pleats from a dropped waist.

5   Baggy shorts were a popular summer alternative. The long length allowed people of all shapes and sizes to wear them, including many who would have looked better in a nice cotton skirt. A stretch-cotton vest is worn under a short-sleeved open shirt tied at the waist.

6   Oversized pink sweatshirt with shoulder pads, raglan sleeves and logo, worn with leggings and headband.

Occasion wear

1   Tailored cocktail or dinner dress in jewel-coloured moiré acetate taffeta. This dress is quite complicated with its criss-cross back detail, padded shoulders and flared basque. Such dresses were inspired by the look created for such actresses as Joan Collins in *Dynasty*. It didn't originate from the Paris or Milan couturiers. It certainly touched a cord with many women, however, as, unlike seventies evening wear, it was assertive, glitzy and ostentatiously glamorous, needing properly done make-up, high heels and tidy hair.

2   Straight crêpe dress with huge shoulders and dolman sleeves decorated with sequinned flowers. The hair is dressed with a fan-like arrangement.

3   An endlessly variable style that has never gone out of fashion: sleeveless top and soft pleat-top pants, worn with a straight jacket in a glamorous beaded or brocaded silk.

4   Beading and sequins became very popular owing to inexpensive imports from the Far East or, rather, western manufacturers took their designs to India or Thailand and had them made up by outworkers for a quarter of the cost. This dress in beaded chiffon hangs from a pleated yoke and is caught by a diamanté buckle on one hip. The full-circle georgette skirt has a flattering asymmetric hem. As the proportion of larger women grew, they at last demanded proper recognition as a fashion force. It was still difficult for them to find glamorous clothes but, for the first time since the days when women had their clothes made for them by dressmakers, it was at least possible.

5   Tailored cocktail suit in ribbed ottoman silk with jewelled buttons, shaped jacket and short straight skirt, worn with black tights and black court shoes.

1

2

3

4

5

Ecclesiastical

The established Christian churches are undergoing great turmoil in the late twentieth century. The decline in numbers of churchgoers has, to some extent, been balanced by the irresistible rise in fundamentalist sects of all persuasions, interest in Eastern religions and the outer reaches of New Age spirituality.

1   The traditional male parish priest in strict clerical garb may soon become an endangered species. This English parson wears his hair fairly long – to identify with the younger members of his flock – and a single-breasted suit in black or grey with a grey duffle-style overcoat, with a clerical collar for special occasions only.

2   Many nuns whose vocation called them to work in the community, felt that their stylish black habits based on medieval widow's weeds rendered them out of touch and élitist; inappropriate for their mission to the poor. It must have taken considerable courage to abandon – literally – the habit of your entire adult life, grow your hair and face Marks & Spencer's again. One Order has a simple solution: anything from Oxfam, as long as it is blue. This nun has a simple short veil, a cross on a cord and sensible shoes.

3   The greatest change in the Anglican church has been the ordination of women, though in Britain this did not happen until after 1990, overcoming profound and sometimes vitriolic objections from traditionalists and fundamentalists. A woman priest wears vestments basically the same as those of a man, over any kind of dark day clothes.

4   Choir boy/girl. Even the great cathedral choirs are beginning to admit girls, though most are still boys, traditionally attired in a white starched ruff or Eton collar, dark-coloured cassock and white surplice.

5   Lay choristers range from the Gospel singers of the American South to numerous ladies in draughty English parish churches. The usual uniform is a mid-calf-length open-sleeved robe loosely based on an academic gown, a detachable white collar and perhaps a soft square 'Tudor' cap. The English variety looks rather less tidy, does not have 'big' hair and wears less make-up.

Working women

1 Black cloth coat with smart black straw hat trimmed with black and white petersham ribbon; leather gloves and court shoes. Such an ensemble would be worn to a funeral or memorial service. Although the idea of formal mourning clothes has long gone, black is often still worn to the actual ceremony as a mark of respect.

2 Young women wear denim. This jacket is a version of the traditional jeans jacket, with an eighties touch in the shape of the dropped padded shoulders and shaped, extended yoke. It is worn with a tight white tank top, a wide leather belt and a denim skirt which has its fullness gathered into a shapely hip basque.

3 What real people wear is seldom fashionable in the conventional sense of the word. Fashion is usually inconvenient in some way but, occasionally, style and comfort do coincide, as in this long knitted cardigan suit. The jacket is in black and white dogstooth check and is trimmed with black edging. It has a matching short, straight skirt for 'occasions' but is worn here with a longish black pleated skirt and white roll-neck jumper.

4 This commanding figure is one of the persistent images of the eighties. The hair is coiffed in large, carefully fixed waves, set firm with lacquer. Her crisp white shirt is finished at the neck with a soft black ribbon bow. The broad-shouldered double-breasted jacket is cut like a man's but in a black and white check wool mix, and the short, straight skirt, sheer tights and suede court shoes are all black.

5 White shirt blouse trimmed with machine tucks and frilled *broderie anglaise*, here worn with a tight elastic belt and the new shaped trousers, pleated onto a hip yoke and cut fairly full over the hips but tapering at the ankles.

Wedding

1   Weddings were almost the only occasion where it was permissible to forget political correctness and look as feminine and romantic as possible. Young women who lived in jeans or black business suits appeared for the day in romantic confections of cream dupion silk, complete with wreaths of real flowers and long net veils. This quite restrained bride has a beaded bodice and silk shoulder bows.

2   Her bridesmaid wears a cotton voile dress by Liberty of London, trimmed with lace at neck, sleeves and hem.

3   A wedding guest wears a Laura Ashley styled summer dress, with pie-frill collar and puffed sleeves; her large straw hat is trimmed with a matching silk rose and a light-coloured handbag is carried at all times.

4   Specially for the occasion, and possibly under protest, this boy wears a shirt in blue and white Swiss lawn, a clip-on bow tie and white cotton trousers.

5   The principal male participants, that is the groom, best man and father of the bride hire matching dove grey morning suits for the day and try not to look like a chorus line.

Recreation

1 Skate-boarding was a huge international craze, which quickly evolved a distinctive style of dress, for identity and for protection. Helmets were not always worn but did advertise that the wearer was capable of stunts involving somersaults. Guards for knees, elbows and wrists looked good and prevented too many sprains. Canvas ankle boots gave some support while remaining flexible. Otherwise the tops and brightly coloured baggy pants or cut-off jeans were standard, street wear.

2 With the introduction of racing and mountain bikes, cycling stopped being simply a healthy, if sedate, way of getting about and became a Lycra-clad obsession, requiring a total outfit consisting of an aerodynamic fibreglass helmet capable of protecting the temples from a 30 mph fall on hard roads; a mask against pollution; top, undershirt and shorts made of nylon and stretch Lycra, covered with brand names, and special cycling shoes.

3 Going to the gym is the ultimate late-twentieth-century pastime and, naturally, requires a complete set of garments that are completely useless for anything else. I am told that the muscles are only useful for posing as well.

4 Hip hop ragamuffin, or off-duty skate-boarder, wears a baseball cap turned back to front, logo-decorated T-shirt, oversize check shirt, enormous drooping Joe Bloggs jeans and Caterpillar or Kickers suede work boots, accompanied by obligatory Walkman with glued-on headphones.

CHAPTER 10

1990–95 – Pluralism

In order to clarify what I perceived as the major trends of the 1980s, it was inevitable that my concentration on the mainstream should cause me to neglect the tributaries. The 1990s are characterized by such a tangled swirling mass of side streams, backwaters and new springs, that if the mainstream exists at all it is very difficult to see. This chapter will therefore take the form of a list of social groups, of necessity incomplete but hopefully giving some idea of what seems to be going on.

Old money The more aristocratic a person considers herself the less interested in the more extreme designer-fashions she is. The glittering excesses of Versace or La Croix are considered dreadfully vulgar and, if she has even heard of Vivienne Westwood or Jean-Paul Gaultier, she will think their ideas simply silly. Her taste and style has hardly changed for fifteen years, since the days of investment dressing in classic clothes, occasionally enlivened by genuine vintage garments, and sumptuous ball gowns by safe designers such as Katherine Walker or Bellville-Sassoon.

It is quite possible that the upper-class man's clothes haven't changed either, for good tailoring lasts and newness for its own sake is still undesirable. The English gentleman has always tended towards the scruffy and, with reduced expendable income, he may now even be a little down at heel.

New money and media stars – the glitterati This group includes film stars, rich industrialists and almost everyone who has appeared in *Hello!* magazine. They exercise an influence on the style of the era because it is new money that buys the expensive designer clothes from the collections of New York, Paris or Milan. As the Hollywood award ceremony is the ultimate social event for these people, it is hardly surprising that the favoured look is one of sexy display, owing much to exposed and unsupported breasts, clinging chiffon and as much glitter as possible. Hair is nearly always blonde, skilfully highlighted, tights are pale and shoes merely minimal straps with high heels. Mae West would have felt completely at home, if confused by the lack of adequate corsetry.

In their need to defy the effects of ageing, many women, and an increasing number of men, undergo extensive cosmetic surgery backed up by a rigorous diet and a personal trainer. It must be said that as long as the overstretched wind-tunnel effect is avoided, many women in their fifties and early sixties look quite amazing.

Ladies who lunch   Mainly the wealthy wives of business and media tycoons, much concerned with fund raising for charity and the arts. Their favourite designers range from Valentino and Armani to Bill Blass and Oscar de la Renta.

The Suit and the Working Girl   A very large group with a number of splinter groups. Men have returned to traditional sartorial values in order to progress along their chosen career path. A high proportion of businessmen who work in the metropolitan centres are expected to wear conventional suits to the office. Suits are compulsory in banking, real estate offices, accounting, sales, the law and corporation boardrooms. Professional women also wear suits. The immense shoulder pads of the eighties have disappeared but neat skirt and trouser suits, usually in black, are seen in executive offices everywhere. Favoured designs are the diffusion ranges of Armani and Jill Sander, supplemented by clothes from Max Mara, Norma Kamali, Donna Karan, or Nicole Farhi plus carefully selected chain-store buys.

Youth   When not subscribing to one of the most extreme style tribes, most young people dress fairly conventionally, in a unisex mix of jeans, T-shirts, blouson jackets and heavy-soled work boots. Most boys wear their hair very short, most girls keep their hair quite long and look after it well. It is said that, although children as young as thirteen experiment with soft drugs as a matter of course, this generation is very responsible in its attitude to unprotected sex. Virginity, even, is considered quite cool. The fear of Aids has had its effect. As a result, routine sexual display through everyday clothes is remarkable for its absence.

Street Style   I shall not attempt to compete with Ted Polhemus here, and will merely repeat his list of nineties style-tribes to give some idea of the diversity involved: Goths, New Romantics, Perus, Psychobillies, Ragamuffins, Rastafarians, New Age Travellers (who are nineties hippies), Ravers, Acid Jazzers, Indie Kids, Cuties, Grunge Girls, Technos and Cyber Punks. I could go on – Leather Queens, Trannies (transvestites), Diesel Dykes and Lipstic Lesbians, Jocks, Hooray Henrys and Sloanes. The tribes are instantly recognisable to themselves and to each other, their multifarious uniforms conferring the reassurance of belonging in an increasingly fragmented world.

Urban cowboys

Much twentieth-century fashion owes its origin to functional work-wear. This hardly comes as a surprise, since clothes suitable for hard physical work are of necessity simple, hard-wearing and devoid of superfluous decoration; in short, classic. The great American cowboy has had an influence on fashion as far-reaching as his contribution to the movie industry.

Western clothing has taken two distinct forms. The first relates to the cowboy's mythic position in the American psyche: he and his female partner are potent symbols of the pioneer spirit, with its visions of liberty, equality and the other Constitutional values. If Laura Ashley costumed the nostalgic images of an English rural Arcadia, then Ralph Lauren, with his ruffled denim and hand-crafted leather, has performed the same magic for America.

The second influence could perhaps be described as the show-biz version; the 'rhinestone-cowboy', sanitized Hollywood Western stars, such as Roy Rogers and the Lone Ranger, serenaded their faithful horses wearing parti-coloured shirts, fringed suede jackets, and piped jeans tucked into expensive Mexican boots, providing inspiration for a multitude of cowboy wannabes. The singers of Country and Western music are especially inventive, wearing flamboyant costumes so sequinned and befringed that even the ironic Versace designer-cowboy is not more ostentatious.

Three suits and a sweater-set

1   Yves St Laurent. Copies by every manufacturer from Harrods' own to most of the high street chains. The jacket is tailored as carefully as a Savile Row suit and the short straight skirt makes it the inevitable formal daywear for many fashion-conscious women.

2   John Galliano. A cleverly cut jacket, based on a nineteenth-century corset pattern, redefines the glamour of the New Look for the nineties. This is one of Galliano's best-selling suits, which at approximately £2500/$3750 says much for its sexy appeal. The suit is made in small-check black and white fine wool worsted, and is worn without a shirt.

3   Armani's unstructured alternative. It is impossible to overestimate the influence of Georgio Armani on late-twentieth-century fashion. His unstructured, beautifully made suits are high on the wish-lists of all sorts of women. He works with the fabric technicians of Italy and Switzerland to produce state-of-the-art, mostly man-made materials of such subtlety and distinction that, although manufacturers from Los Angeles to Hong Kong shamelessly copy his timeless shapes, none of them comes anywhere near the genuine article.

4   The nineties version of a fifties favourite; the twin- or sweater-set, popular in 1995–6 in a range of citrus or pastel colours; it is worn here with a short, bias-cut viscose satin skirt, reminiscent of the flower print slip dresses of the thirties. As has often been said, all fashion is retro, if you look hard enough.

1

2

3

4

Mail Order

A page of casual wear from Littlewoods home shopping catalogue. Such a catalogue is an excellent indicator of what the majority of people actually wear, as distinct from what the glossy magazine editors think they wear.

1   Crop top in sweatshirt fabric, worn with cotton mix drawstring shorts. This has to be as cheap and simple a solution to sports and beach dressing as can be imagined.

2   Hooded and zipped unisex sports top in the same fleecy fabric as the comfortable jogging pants. It is worn over a vest or body and with canvas shoes or trainers. These are easy natural clothes that require no thought, grooming or care in selection, relying for their appeal entirely on the freshness and condition of the wearer's face and body.

3   Another crop top, this time in corn-coloured knitted viscose, worn with simple drawstring pants in an Indian print cotton. Note the 'cross-cultural' hair. The wearer has some American Indian blood and has done her long hair in tiny beaded braids, more usually associated with African hairstyles.

4   Little knitted top in polycotton with unturned hems made frilly by stretching the fabric as it is passed through the overlocker, thus making a decorative virtue out of a potential mistake. A cotton sun-hat and denim jeans skirt finish this useful ensemble.

5   Long gelled hair is scraped back into a pony tail. Small round sunglasses are worn with the crucial nineties' accessory, the mobile phone. Her T-shirt is nylon with Lycra to ensure a shrunken fit; her short pleated skirt is red and white striped polyester.

6   A teenage uniform of black padded nylon zippered jacket, V-neck sweater and baggy jeans.

1

2

3

4

5

6

Shoes

1   Moccasins with the popular 1995 clumpy heel. Shoes for women are polarized between delicate, strappy shoes for occasion wear and heavy-duty functionalism for everything else. These moccasin styles are offered in every material from black patent to *faux* snakeskin with a see-through plastic sole and heel.

2   Simple court shoes with a pretty low heel, in black, navy or taupe, are worn by women who wish to look neat and feminine in the workplace and for semi-formal day wear.

3   High heels are back for dressy occasions; for some, they never went away. This example with flattering, slightly waisted heel and crossed straps is worn to 'feminize' a serious suit or to finish the look of a black cocktail dress. Pale tights are fashionable but many women persist in the belief that black is more flattering.

4   Built-up canvas shoes, an inexpensive and popular option for the young. This version is offered in gold Lurex, as well as the season's colours.

5   The eight-hole work boot by Doc Marten defines mid-nineties urban Britain. These everlasting, over-sized, comfortable boots are seen everywhere in black with jeans or opaque black tights and are as ubiquitous and as genuinely unisex as jeans. They can also be found in colours or tartans, even in leather printed with sparkly holograms.

6   Knee-high laced boot with a solid medium-height heel; it looks good with skirts of any length but is sometimes seen with leggings or stretch jeans.

7   The walking sandal with heavy moulded composition soles and carefully placed wide fabric straps is one of the few footwear developments of the nineties. Comfortable sandals, once known rudely as 'Jesus creepers' and worn principally by earnest moralists or middle-aged bohemians, are now a serious warm-weather option for both sexes – and if not exactly fashionable, are nevertheless extremely popular.

8   This much-copied laced moccasin by Timberland in green and brown waxed leather is widely worn as a casual shoe.

9   Another Doc Marten shoe, much worn by school children with or without the integral steel toe-cap. They are not glamorous but at least the young now have beautifully straight toes and mothers approve because they never wear out.

10   A rather peculiar earth shoe with crepe sole and unfinished hide upper. With its square toe and primitive styling, it could be peasant footwear from almost any period.

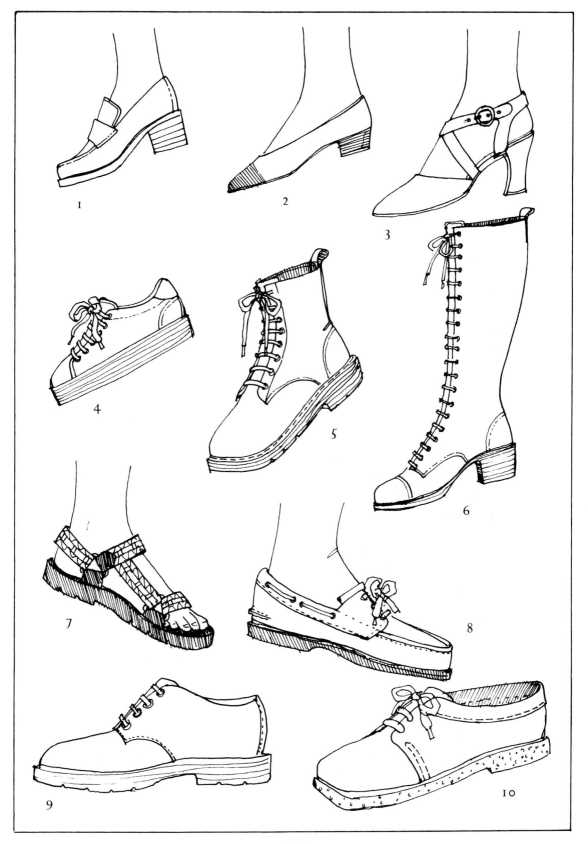

New men

1   It is not really true that all men in the mid nineties look as if they are dressed as lumberjacks but, out of doors, men who don't wear the middle-class outer uniform of Barbour jacket, tweeds and wellies, certainly try. This carefully designed all-season weather coat has a fleecy zip-in body warmer for winter, a hood concealed in the collar, and is wind- and waterproof. Originally designed for serious mountaineers, such garments have infiltrated all levels of society and can even be seen over city suits on the streets of London and New York. This chap wears a 'granddad' shirt, jeans and serious, two- or even three-tone suede and leather walking boots.

2   The alternative weather-coat for those who dislike the class affiliations of green waxed Barbour jackets and who feel that anoraks of any description, however over-designed, are for nerds: the Australian 'horse rustler's favourite' called Drizabone has a shoulder-cape, warm check lining and a split pleat in the back to fit neatly over your horse's rump. It is usually made in brown waxed cotton.

3   The designer option: black glasses, tie-less shirt, belt, slacks and shoes, here worn with a beautifully tailored light grey jacket. The medium length hair is gelled back.

1

2

3

Underwear

1   Most women prefer not to go bra-less but this strange hybrid garment will provide some support. It is an all-in-one nylon under-body or teddy, wired under the bust and poppered under the crotch. Though it has a certain sexy charm on its own, it is uncomfortable and inconvenient in wear.

2   Cool and functional, if deliberately downbeat, set in denim marl cotton and Lycra. The bra is efficiently uplifting in the Wonderbra style, but the panties look like old-fashioned games knickers to me – though it would be comforting to know that you can have your cleavage and be politically correct.

3   The breasts that remain after all that working out and dieting often need more tactful support than they did before, hence the need for the specially designed sports bra. This one has a 'racing' back, air vents, wide, comfortable straps and elastic under the bust. You still bounce, though. Lycra and cotton knee-length shorts were originally designed for competition cyclists but are now seen every-where for sports and leisure wear. Sexy on the perfectly toned, they can look positively frightening on the stout.

4   The night-shirt has become an object for all kinds of marketing exercises. This one in black and white confines itself to teddy bears, but they can be found advertising anything from baseball teams to Winnie-the-Pooh.

5   The obsession with fitness has spawned whole stores devoted to exercise clothing. Here a pink cap-sleeved, thong-back body is worn with toning striped leggings.

6   One-piece swimsuit with a famous logo woven across its chest. Note the very high-cut leg and the modest tank-top straps.

High fashion in the USA

1   Armani in Atlanta. Perfect long-line brocade jacket with double lettuce-edge chiffon skirt. Wealthy American women dress up far more than their British counterparts, and West Coast and especially Texan women wear more expensive sparkly clothes than anyone else.

2   Jackie O-style sleeveless dress and tailored jacket by Ralph Lauren. A bit dull for Los Angeles but popular in New York and London.

3   Showy black slip dress with lace insertions by Calvin Klein. This dress is considered too vulgar for Southern ladies but is also much liked in New York and Los Angeles.

1

2

3

Showbiz

1   Very grand American evening dress. A pink panné velvet cardigan is worn here with an 1870s-inspired enormous pink and gold silk bustle skirt and big blonde hair.

2   Any one of the dresses on this page is grand and glittery enough to attend the Oscar ceremony, neatly demonstrating the polarization of late-twentieth-century fashion. This strapless shiny red dress has an intricately draped top mounted on a firmly boned bodice and a gathered skirt.

3   The classic Awards Ceremony dress has hardly changed since Mae West wiggled into shot trussed into champagne sequins, with blonde hair and the highest heels she could stand up in. Actress Tippi Hendren wears a fairly re-strained version in sea-green beaded chiffon with its halter neckline cleverly cut to accommodate the firm corsetry but the skirt slashed to the thigh to reveal a still beautiful leg.

4   I have tried to avoid a judgemental tone in these pages, but the idea behind this particular outfit quite eludes me. It was worn to a 'themed' costume ball in Hollywood but seems to have three quite separate themes. An exquisitely embroidered cream and gold corset is worn with a tight split lilac-pink skirt. The lady's modesty is preserved with a brown silk organza jacket with split kimono-like sleeves, the whole thing topped with an expertly dressed chignon and shod with nude tights and leopard-print stiletto heels.

5   Another classic 'full dress' look. A long white sequinned gown with tiny shoulder straps and a fitted waist looks modern because of the tumbling blonde hair and the well-exercised body beneath. The vast stole adds casual glamour.

1

2

3

4

5

Street clothes

1   I thought this was an example of grunge but I am told it is 'cutie'. The ladies of Atlanta, indeed anyone over thirty, would be appalled by this image. Warm-weather functional clothes were always a bit of a problem. Here a cotton high-waisted tank-top dress is worn over a vest (tank top). The girl carries an 'ethnic' cloth bag and wears a woven friendship bracelet, round dark glasses, the in-evitable black DMs and bare legs.

2   A couple of revellers from a Shampoo Planet Club event. She has done her bleached hair in foil-wrapped sections, her black sheath dress (vinyl? bin liner?) is held up by a studded collar, and her mittens are made from what looks like hold-up black socks. He has dyed his spiky hair scarlet to match his T-shirt and velvet hipster trousers. I think the cropped fun fur jacket must belong to his friend.

3   How much more extreme can one get? A shaven head was once a badge of ultimate shame, reserved for concentration camp victims and wartime collabor-ators. This is really how to upset your mother: a scalp blue with cold and all-over five o'clock shadow combined with multiple earrings, nose-studs and, most painful of all, an eyebrow ring.

4   London Rastafarian, Brixton-style. An over-sized crochet hat controls the long dreadlocks.

5   A popular no-fashion look for the young when not wearing jeans. Calf-length button-through dress in flower-sprigged viscose worn over a brief T-shirt and probably black boots or canvas shoes.

6   Young man in a gay bar. He wears a black paramilitary beret, several silver earrings in one ear, studded bulldog collar, black nylon jacket with sleeves cut off, a tattoo, tight frayed denim jeans and combat boots.

CHAPTER 11

Towards the Millennium

Something very strange has happened in fashion during the last two years. Revivals have come round ever sooner in the twentieth century, as designers become increasingly desperate for a new image, and 1996 sees a vigorous revival of the 1960s Jackie Kennedy/Audrey Hepburn look. What is unusual about this one is that the little sleeveless shifts and matching coats, the button-up cardigans and pale shoes are almost identical to the day clothes that the original followers of the style have never stopped wearing for formal occasions.

The glossy magazines make them look quite different from the sixties originals, I suspect because the clothes themselves are only interesting if presented in a very extreme way. The late nineties' look is that of a bleached super-waif with a chemically-induced hangover, the inevitable reaction to the eighties' super-fit bronzed Californian body-builder.

The clever girl will often have found a sixties original in a charity shop or vintage clothing store, combining new and old with great aplomb. My fourteen-year-old daughter, for instance, found a smart late sixties caramel-coloured fitted thigh-length coat which she wears with a Benetton skinny-rib turtle-neck, her friend's Gap hipsters and chunky-heeled loafers. Her elder sister, aged nineteen, found a beautiful long white slubbed silk evening dress in a King's Road vintage clothing boutique, complete with a chiffon midriff decorated with a crystal fringe, which she wore with great success to an extremely grand dinner, where it fitted in perfectly with the older generations' designer clothes for a tenth of the price.

This chapter is intended as both a summing up and a point of departure; neither is easily achieved, as the subject is too enormous, too slippery to submit to simplistic analysis, so I will make some pronouncements, which will lead to their own necessarily tentative conclusions.

We all belong to one or more style tribes, consciously or by virtue of class, activity or occupation. Everything I said in chapter 10 about groups is still in place; the changes seem to apply to small bands of fashion groupies but, as has happened in the past, the filter-down effect will see them adopted more generally.

All fashion is retro now. It's difficult to argue with this. Certainly much so-called new design is a witty reworking of the old, a reassembling of bits and pieces put together with a modern slant to reflect the prevailing *zeitgeist*.

1996 is the year of Geek Chic, so we are told. A *Vogue* editorial is embarrassed to state that purple crimplene slacks, shirts in shower-curtain print nylon, worn with plaid A-line mini skirts, Hush Puppie shoes and a plastic lunch box for a bag is cool – (or do I mean hot?). These ironic clothes are intentionally 'off', the idea is that it is un-cool to look too pretty or feminine. Unfortunately, as with grunge fashion, people who are not in the know may think this deliberate nerdiness is just plain unattractive (NB this category includes ninety-five per cent of men, most European women, American women – apart from the trendy Urban Fashion victims, and anyone over the age of thirty).

Eighty per cent of the clothing worn by the population of the industrialized countries is not fashion at all. The great majority of men and women acquire their clothes from the multi-national chain stores, from department stores and from catalogues, most people trying to steer a middle course between the new and the out-of-date. Their choice of clothes is governed by suitability for the individual's preferred life style, and cost. English women are traditionally at the bottom of the league table when it comes to spending on fashion, with Belgians at the top. German women would not be seen dead in a charity shop, whereas garments from the 'Donated by the Stars' thrift shop in Los Angeles are very smart indeed.

Clothes are ever more clearly defined by life style and activity, in a way that mostly ignores the twice-yearly changes of high fashion. Few people dress up in the evening now but, when they do, the fashion statements are often extreme. One only has to read the gossip magazines and then look around at ordinary people to see evidence of this.

To look expensive costs as much money as it always did. Designer outfits start at £2,000 or so, and the accompanying hairdressing, face lifts, designer accessories and beauty treatments cost an immense investment of time and effort as well as cash. The only people who defy this statement are the very young, who look wonderful anyway; the exceptionally beautiful who will either borrow, or have a sugar-daddy – or increasingly nowadays sugar-mummy – buy it for them, and the clever few who can design, make or find their own off-beat ensembles. This latter category must usually content themselves with looking interesting instead of expensive.

The increase in homosexuality of both sexes, combined with the feminization of men. I am in dangerous waters here, but the facts speak for themselves. The revealed incidence of male homosexuality in the West has increased enormously since 1945 and continues to rise.

Tracing a parallel trajectory to the rise of male homosexuality is the phenomenon of transvestism, otherwise known as cross-dressing or drag. I am not concerned here with those who dress in clothes opposite to their gender because of a conviction that they have been born in the wrong body, or with those heterosexual men who by shedding masculine costume seek to liberate themselves from the expectations of a still-paternalistic society. The archetype I wish to consider is the rise of the drag artiste. From underground perform-ances in sleazy drinking clubs by sad men who could only connect with an audience when dressed as women, to the joyous sophisticated performers who appear in the grandest of mainstream venues, the favourite images are usually drawn from the most extreme icons of femininity, Mae West, Marilyn Monroe, and latterly Dolly Parton. By the time the man has plucked and waxed the unwanted body hair, padded the breast, bottom and hips, corseted the waist, applied expert makeup, finished with a clinging sequin dress, high heels and a towering blonde wig he will be a sex goddess indeed, even surpassing the original icon herself in extravagant glittering allure.

Even as recently as the 1980s it would have been quite inconceivable that an exclusive advertising contract with a mainstream cosmetic company should have gone to a seven-foot-tall black man with big hair and fuck-me pumps – to wit, Ru Paul.

Lead stories in several responsible newspapers recently have combined with television programmes to inform us that male fertility has dropped be-tween twenty and forty per cent in two generations. Many causes have been suggested for this discovery, ranging from the rise of the power of women to the leaching of oestrogen-like compounds into our drinking water. Are these statistics Creation's way of limiting the population, or are we evolving into Plato's ideal of the perfect human being, half man and half woman? And if the answer to either or both of these questions is in the affirmative, will this new gender stand a chance of survival against old-fashioned war-like Man, who is still bloodily dominant in much of the Planet?

18. Dressy black suit for
the nineties 1991

19. Thirty-five years of
Chanel – 1961, 1989 and 1996

20. Mrs Steer and her granddaughter 1994

22. Girl and boy waifs in the
citrus colours for geeks 1996

23. Corset and bum-bag
by Designer of the Year,
Vivienne Westwood, 1995

Postscript

Feeling excluded from the happening edge of street style, I asked Gregory Dean, a student at Lancaster University who expressed interest in this book, for a commentary on youth, fashion and the post-modern attitude. It is so helpful that I include it in full:

'Contemporary youth or "street" style is an incredibly complex and undocumented phenomenon. It might be helpful to look at its relationship with the world of *Vogue* and the catwalks in terms of "anti-fashion" and "fashion".

'Clothing can be seen as a way of communicating values to do with the self, cultural values and social identity. Youth culture since the fifties has been largely concerned with rebellion, expressing difference and dissatisfaction, a separation from older generations' values and traditions. Clothes are, of course, an ideal medium in which to assert this difference, hence "anti-fashion", youth's attempt to adopt clothing styles that disrupt and contradict contemporary mainstream fashion, setting their wearers visibly apart.

'The fashion of difference in the UK is most apparent in movements such as skinheads, Teddy boys and punks. Punk is believed to have been the final expression of the dissatisfied youth group; nothing after it could match its mix of extreme ugliness, adrogyny, peacockery and aggression. After punk, a youth look or anti-fashion would never have the same effect.

'The major problem concerning "anti-fashion" has been its hijack and use by mainstream fashion. Anti-fashion, almost by definition, carries with it connotations of rebelliousness, coolness and relevance, all characteristics now sought after by the major fashion chainstores. Designers have become increasingly aware of and in tune with anti-fashion, and use it to influence their collections to such an extent that the notion of anti-fashion is becoming meaningless. An example of this is that major clothing chainstores employ "spotters" to report any new trend in the anti-fashion set which they then translate into mass-produced cheap copies.

'Pluralism, perhaps the defining feature of post-modern society, has also soiled the aims of anti-fashion. When everything is equally relevant and valid, what is there left to rebel against or shock with? It is, perhaps, a crowning achievement of this rebellion that nowadays "anything goes"; but with coolness and rebellion inextricably linked, how can coolness be attainable now that fashion can no longer be rebellious?

'The consequences of these factors for the anti-fashion élite and the scenesters are evident in, as far as I can see, three different phenomena. Firstly, an increased rate of revivalism, in an attempt to outdo the cashing in on each new movement by the mass media and major designers – we are currently in the process of a third mod revival, countless "new" sixties and seventies revivals surface every few months, and in 1996 (something no one could have expected a year or so ago) a "New Romantic" mid-eighties revival. This last example is proof, I think, of fashion's ever accelerating capacity to consume and regurgitate itself in order to give itself life. Needless to say, all these revivals require an increasing sense of post-modern irony in their wearers.

'The second result is that the élite (probably only a few hundred people) have adopted a ludicrously exclusive and cliquey attitude in order to stay ahead. In an article in the English magazine *The Face*, Frazer Cooke, a self-confessed fashion victim, recounted how he and his set would ship over clothing by Stüssy and Nike from America and Japan months before they hit the stores and then would cut off the labels as the only way to remain different, ahead of the game and therefore "cool". These few hundred are the club runners, DJs, alternative journalists and music scene people who are so influential in the whole anti-fashion/fashion system. The close relationship of music with youth fashion is another vital ingredient in youth identity, too complex to explore here.

'Thirdly, and relating to music, is the huge diversity of different styles and codes (a product of the pluralist climate) that youth can now buy into. Every new music style has spawned its respective fashion, among which are Raver, New Romantic, B-Boy, Goth, Acid Jazzer, the Indie Look, Mod, Romo, Grunge, Hip-Hop, Rastafarian (no longer just a religion, its dreadlocks and clothes hijacked by white agnostics), Traveller and Junglist. All denote a different look for youth to choose from. "A supermarket of styles" has been the phrase used to label this phenomenon. In the last couple of years pluralism has reached such an extent that one can now pick elements of clothing out of these styles and mix and match them. For instance, a pair of "old school" trainers (product of the early eighties hip-hop style) could be worn with tight, mod-influenced, cords and a Stüssy baggy top (originally made for skateboarders). The wearer might have dreadlocks (but no Rastafarian beliefs). This type of get-up might be seen on any high street, a proof of just how fragmented and complicated youth fashion has become.'

Glossary

angora (1) Hair of angora goat, used in making mohair. (2) Hair of angora rabbit used as a very soft knitting wool for women's sweaters.

appliqué French for 'applied' or 'laid on'; decoration in the form of embroidery, cut-out motif or contrasting fabrics stitched onto a base fabric.

atelier French for studio or work shop; a designer's work-room where designs are created and made up.

bandanna (1) Hindu word for a dyeing process. (2) A large patterned handkerchief worn round the head or neck.

bandeau Narrow band worn around the head.

barathea Smooth wool or wool and polyester fabric, origin-ally used for uniforms and men's dinner jackets, now used as a high-quality suiting material.

Barbour jacket English country weather-coat made from waterproof waxed cotton.

basque A short flared piece of fabric attached to the bodice at the waist (cf. Peplum); a short-skirted jacket.

bateau neck boat-shaped, slightly curved neckline.

batik Method of applying dyed designs to fabric by successive coatings of the fabric with wax, so that with each dipping only the uncovered parts take the dye.

batwing sleeve Long sleeve with an armhole cut to the waist and narrow at the wrist.

bias cut Fabric cut at 45 degrees to the selvedge. This causes the garment to hang in a very fluid and graceful way.

block (1) A mould used to make and shape a hat. (2) An orig-inal card pattern cut without seam allowances.

boater Flat straw hat with a straight brim and ribbon trim, originally worn by both sexes in the summer during the early years of the twentieth century.

bodice The part of a dress from the shoulder to the waist.

bolero Short jacket worn open in the front, finishing above the waist.

bowler hat Formal man's hat in stiffened black felt with a domed crown and narrow curled brim, popular with English 'city gents'.

braces Suspenders (US).

braid (1) Narrow strip of flat tape for trimming and binding. (2) In US, a plait of hair.

brocade Jaquard weave fabric with all-over raised pattern often incorporating foliage or flowers.

broderie anglaise Embroidery of small, often floral patterns punched or cut, then oversewn. Normally of white cotton and used as a border or frill on lingerie.

buckram Loosely-woven cotton heavily starched with glue size, used for stiffening garments and hats.

calico Plain woven cotton originally from Calicut, India. Manufactured in various weights, calico is used to make trial versions of complex garments so as not to waste expensive fabric.

camisole Light under-bodice with straight-cut top on narrow shoulder straps.

cap sleeve Short grown-on sleeve just covering the top of the arm.

cardigan Loose knitted jacket, supposedly named after Lord Cardigan.

cashmere Soft luxurious cloth made from the under-hair of Himalayan goats.

Chantilly lace Bobbin lace with a fine background and de-signs outlined with silk thread.

cheese cloth Thin, unsized, slightly crinkly cotton, much used for ethnic tops and skirts.

chemise Loose shirtlike undergarment or shift, now more commonly a straight unbelted dress in soft material.

chenille Silk, cotton or rayon fabric with a tufted velvet-like pile woven in fine ridges (from the French word for cater-pillar).

chiffon Transparent floaty fabric woven from silk, rayon or polyester.

choker Short necklace or fitted collar that clasps the neck like a dog collar.

classic Clothing that remains stylish because of its essential simplicity; not owing anything to passing trends.

cloche A close-fitting bell-shaped hat.

coat-dress Tailored front-fastening dress made in the style of a lightweight coat.

cocktail dress Short semi-formal evening dress, designed to be worn during the cocktail hour.

coiffure Arrangement of the hair, usually elaborate.

corduroy, cord Cotton or polycotton cutpile fabric with variable width ribbing.

corsage A bouquet of real or artificial flowers worn as decor-ation at shoulder, breast or waist.

corset Figure-moulding, supportive undergarment, stiffened with steel, whalebone or (nowadays) plastic strips. Originally fastened with laces; they gave period costume its distinctive shape.

corselette Modern lightweight corset-like undergarment, usually made from nylon lace, satin and elastic.

costume jewelry Jewelry made from non-precious metals and stones, usually more ostentatious than the real thing, and comparatively inexpensive.

couture French for dressmaking; now used to mean the top or made-to-measure end of the fashion spectrum.

couturier A top international fashion designer.

cravat A shaped silky scarf worn folded about the neck instead of a tie.

crepe Material woven so that the surface resembles the skin of an orange; usually having a pleasing matte bloom, made from silk, wool, rayon or polyester.

crushed velvet Heat and pressure treated so that the surface is irregular and distressed.

Cuban heel Medium chunky, slightly tapering heel, as seen on cowboy boots.

culottes Very flared trousers cut to fall together to give the appearance of a skirt.

cut The way in which a garment is shaped, how it hangs.

decolleté Low-cut neckline exposing the shoulder and upper part of the breasts, usually a bodice style for evening wear.

dirndl Full, straight-cut skirt gathered onto a waistband.

dolman sleeve Sleeve with a deep armhole, and gathered at the wrist; cut in one piece with the body.

Donegal tweed Homespun slubbed wool cloth originally woven by Irish crofters.

double-breasted Type of front for a coat or jacket, which overlaps sufficiently to allow for two rows of buttons.

drape (1) To hang fabric in loose folds. (2) To create a dress on the body or stand using this method.

dummy Model or dress-form used to work on the unfinished garment or to display the completed one.

duster coat Lightweight unlined wrap coat.

Empire line Named after the fashions of the Empress Josephine; a high-waisted line with the skirt falling straight from immediately below the bust.

ensemble Used to describe a complete outfit.

espadrille Rope-soled shoe with a canvas upper, for casual summer wear.

Eton collar A high, slightly flared, turned down stiff collar.

eyelet Small hole or perforation edged with stitching or a small metal reinforcement; used as decoration or, when threaded with a cord, as a method of fastening.

facing Visible lining for those parts of a garment that are turned outward in wear, such as lapels and collars.

Fair Isle Traditional knitwear patterned with small multi-coloured geometric designs, named from the Scottish island.

fedora Wide-brimmed, soft felt hat with a crease running from the front to the back of the crown, as worn by Hollywood gangsters.

felt Non-woven fabric formed by treating fibres with heat and pressure, much used for hats, and occasionally for decorative cut and appliqué work.

filigree Very delicate, open, lace-like fabric.

finish (1) The surface of fabric after treatment such as embossing, napping or glazing. (2) The standard of workmanship in a garment.

flannel Soft wool fabric with a slight nap.

flannelette Soft brushed cotton fabric used to make nightwear.

flounce A gathered frill sewn onto a garment, found mostly on underskirts.

gabardine Twilled, worsted coating used for raincoats, uniforms, or riding habits.

gilet French for waistcoat or decorated vest.

gingham Lightweight cotton woven into checks, usually in a single colour and white.

girdle Elasticized undergarment worn to flatten the tummy and buttocks.

godet Triangular segment of cloth set into a skirt or sleeve to create fullness.

gore Flared section of fabric, narrow at the waist and wide at the hem, to create shapely skirts without excess fabric at the waist.

grain The direction of warp and woof threads in a woven fabric. Most garments are cut 'on the straight' (of the grain) so that they hang properly and don't drop out of shape. Fabric cut 'on the bias' is more fluid and clingy, as seen in the romantic, floppy dresses of the nineteen-thirties.

grown-on Sleeves, collars etc. cut in one with main garment.

gusset Triangular or diamond-shaped piece of fabric let into a garment to adjust the fit or give extra ease to a tight armhole.

halter neckline Strap around the neck attached to the front of the bodice to support a low-backed dress.

harem pants Full, draped trousers gathered to fit at the ankle.

Harris tweed Soft but exceptionally hardwearing wool tweed originally woven on the island of Harris on the west coast of Scotland.

haute couture High fashion, always made to measure.

hobble skirt Long skirt, narrow at the ankles, which restricts walking.

hound's-tooth check Small pattern of broken checks.

jabot Frilled or pleated piece of fabric attached to the front of the neckline, often trimmed with lace.

jerkin Long-line vest or waistcoat, usually cut straight or only semi-fitted.

jersey (1) Plain knit, finely ribbed fabric with some elasticity made from cotton, silk, wool, etc. (2) Unstructured pullover made from jersey fabric, or knitted.

jodhpurs Trousers cut full over the thighs but fitting tightly from knee to ankle. Originally worn for horse riding as less formal alternative to breeches and knee-high boots.

kapok Fibre from the silk-cotton tree, used as padding in quilted garments; now usually replaced by polyester wadding.

knickerbockers Full-cut pants or breeches fastened at the knee.

knife pleats Narrow pleats, often permanently pressed; popular for school uniform skirts.

lace Can be hand- or machine-made, narrow for trimming, or wide for making a complete garment. There are many different types of machine-made lace, but it normally consists of a net base decorated with embroidery in silk, cotton or lurex.

lamé Fabric made from metallic threads.

leotard Tight-fitting 'body' or all-in-one, made from cotton or nylon and Lycra, worn mostly by dancers.

loafer Casual slip-on shoe with a low heel, based on the moccasin of the native American.

loden Overcoat cut to fall loosely from a shoulder yoke, made in dark green or charcoal Loden cloth, a thick waterproof woollen fabric.

Lurex Trade name for a glittery yarn made by coating aluminium foil with coloured plastic film.

Lycra Trade name for a durable stretchy man-made fibre. It is mixed with a wide variety of other yarns to add shapeliness without complex seaming.

macramé A fringe or trimming made from knotted string or soft cotton yarn.

mandarin collar Narrow straight collar that stands up from the fitted neckline of a jacket or dress.

moccasin Heelless shoe made from a single piece of leather gathered on top of the foot.

model (1) A person who displays clothes by posing for photographers, journalists and potential customers. (2) A garment which serves as a pattern or sample. (3) A high-quality designer garment made to order in limited quantities, and carrying the designer's label.

moleskin Heavy cotton brushed to a suede-like finish, used to make men's work clothes.

needlecord Fine-rib corduroy.

negligée A decorative full-length dressing robe.

nylon A synthetic yarn or fabric made from coal; it is washable, elastic and easily dyed.

opera cloak A full-length evening cloak.

Oxford A low-cut man's shoe with front-laced fastening.

Oxford bags Very wide men's trousers, with the fullness pleated into the waistband.

Panama hat Man's fedora-shaped hat made from fine foldable straw from Panama.

panné velvet Velvet rendered smooth and shiny by pressing all the fibres in the same direction.

pea-jacket Loose double-breasted jacket based on those traditionally worn by fishermen.

pedal-pushers Trousers ending just below the knee, suitable for cycling.

pencil skirt A narrow straight skirt.

peplum A ruffle extending from the waist seam to hip level.

Peter Pan collar A soft turn-down collar with rounded ends.

petticoat Woman's underskirt or slip, often trimmed with lace or frills.

picture hat Lady's wide-brimmed straw hat, often trimmed with ribbons and flowers.

plus-fours Wide-cut knickerbockers, fastening at the knee with a four-inch over-fold.

polo-neck A collar style consisting of a tube of fabric rolled to the required height.

polo shirt Short-sleeved sport shirt in knitted jersey.

prêt-à-porter Ready to wear.

pyjamas Loose unstructured lounging suit, originally for beach or sleep wear.

raffia Straw made from palm fibre, used to make and decorate summer hats and bags.

raglan sleeve A deep-cut sleeve with the armhole extending to the neckline.

raw silk Rough silk fabric made from the outer cocoons of the silk-worm.

rayon Man-made fabric manufactured from processed cellulose.

rick-rack Coloured zig-zag braid used to decorate gypsy-style clothes.

roll collar Similar to the polo neck, but made to stand away from the neck.

rompers All-in-one child's garment, consisting of a bib top attached to short bloused knickers.

sack A dress cut straight from shoulder to hem designed to fit where it touches; usually knee length.

sarong Wide, brightly printed length of cotton that is wound round the body to make a simple ankle-length skirt.

sash An ornamental band or scarf, worn round head, shoulders, or more usually, waist.

sequin A small metal disc of any colour used for decoration of evening clothes. The paillete is the same thing in any shape other than circular.

shawl collar One-piece, usually grown-on unnotched collar.

sheath A straight, tight-fitting dress.

shift A straight shirt or blouse-like dress (originally an undergarment).

shirtwaister A dress cut like an elongated shirt, with a tightly belted waist.

singlet Sleeveless, low-necked sport shirt; tank top (US).

slacks Loosely fitting, pleat-front trousers.

slip A simple petticoat worn to improve the hang of a dress.

sloppy Joe Oversized slip-on sweater or jumper.

smock Originally a shepherd's work garment, cut like an oversized shirt and gathered onto a yoke.

smocking A form of decoration where the evenly gathered fabric is overstitched in a traditional series of patterns.

sneaker A casual canvas rubber-soled shoe with central front lacing.

sombrero A straw hat with a high crown and a very wide brim.

sou'wester A waterproof fisherman's hat, with the brim wider at the back than at the front.

stiletto heel A very pointed high heel like a stiletto dagger.

stole A long wide evening scarf used as shoulder wrap.

swagger coat A coat cut to hang in a bold flare from the shoulders.

sweater A knitted pullover top.

sweatshirt A casual knitted cotton-mix top, often fleeced, with a round neck and long sleeves.

tam-o'-shanter A sort of full beret with a bobble on the top.

terry cloth Towelling fabric.

tie-dye A method of creating dyed patterns by pleating and twisting the fabric, then tying it at intervals so tightly that the colour cannot penetrate the tied bits.

train An extended panel, usually of a wedding dress, that trails behind the wearer.

trench coat A generously cut weather-coat with many flaps and pockets, belted at the waist.

T-shirt Sport or undershirt, usually made from cotton jersey.

turtle neck High-fitted neckline for jumpers or pullovers; another name for roll or polo neck.

twinset (US Sweater set) A short-sleeved fitted sweater worn with matching button-through cardigan.

velour Woven, knit or felted fabric having a thick velvet pile.

vest (1) singlet or undergarment (UK). (2) American name for waistcoat.

waistcoat English for US vest.

wedge heel Solid heel made as a continuation of the sole.

wellington boots Originally a type of thigh boot cut down to knee level at the back, presumably for greater comfort when on a horse. Now a calf-covering, one-piece rubber boot.

winceyette Soft brushed cotton fabric used for nightwear.

windbreaker/windcheater Outdoor jacket made of proofed cotton or wool and having an elasticized hemband at the waist or hip.

yoke A fitted shoulder-piece from which the rest of the garment hangs.

Bibliography

Costume and Fashion: A Concise History
JAMES LAVER Thames and Hudson, London 1969

Everyday Fashions of the Forties: as Pictured in Sears Catalogs
JOANNE OLIAN Dover Books, New York 1992

Fabric of Society
JANE TOZER and SARAH LEVITT
Laura Ashley Publications 1983

Fashion in Costume, 1200–1980
JOAN NUNN The Herbert Press, London 1984

Fashion, the Mirror of History
MICHAEL and ARIANE BATTERSBY
Columbus Books, London 1977

The Fifties in Vogue
NICHOLAS DRAKE Henry Holt, New York 1987

In Vogue: Seventy-five Years of Style
GEORGINA HOWELL Condé Nast/Century, London 1991

McDowell's Directory of 20th-Century Fashion
COLIN McDOWELL Muller, London 1984

Maternity Fashion
DORETTA DAVANZO POLI Zanfi Editori, Italy 1988

Parkinson's Photographs, 1935 to 1990
MARTIN HARRISON Conran Octopus, London 1994

Pictorial History of the 20th Century
Hamilton, London 1989

The Royal Portraits
CECIL BEATON Thames and Hudson, London 1988

Streetstyle
TED POLHEMUS Thames and Hudson, New York 1994

Index